Secrets in the Mist

The History of Brown's Island
Weirton, West Virginia

JANE KRAINA
and
MARY ZWIERZCHOWSKI

Edited by Dwight McUmar

Copyright © 2022 Jane Kraina
All rights reserved

ISBN 13 (paperback): 979-8-9854945-0-1
ISBN (ebook): 979-8-9854945-1-8

Disclaimer: A variety of viewpoints are presented in this history and the views and opinions are solely those of those who were interviewed and do not represent opinions or viewpoints of the authors. We have not been able to present complete written documentation on some of the causes of the events. For this reason, we have not put forth official answers to some of the questionable causes of the explosion. We have offered several scenarios told to us. We do not endorse any one viewpoint.

Dedication

*To the hundreds of workers, whose labor –
both skilled and unskilled – built the coke plant at Brown's Island,
in connection with Weirton Steel Corporation and Koppers Company,
we dedicate this book.*

In Memory Of:

The nineteen men, whose lives were lost in the Brown's Island coke plant explosion. December 15, 1972. You are not forgotten.

Charles Bowers
Howard Bray
James Brown
Paul Byrne
Michael Crowley
Edward "Dick" Arthurs
Kenny Gaines
Kenneth Harris
William Kliner
Andy Guz
Arthur McCort
Samuel Morgart
Russell Ober
Michael Repko
Lou Sommers
Albert Tuttle
James Tuttle
John Toms
David Van Sickle

A Note to Readers

Some historical and geographical points
- West Virginia was part of Virginia until 1863.
- Ohio County made up all the northern panhandle of Virginia (now West Virginia) until 1796. At that time the land was divided, and the upper part became Brooke County. In 1848 it further split so that Hancock became the northernmost part, Brooke the middle and Ohio County the southern part.

Town name changes
- **West Virginia**
    - Holliday's Cove became part of Weirton in 1947.
    - Charlestown was the original name of Wellsburg
- **Ohio**
    - Ohio became a state in 1803 and was known as the Ohio Country before that
- **Pennsylvania**
    - Catfish Camp became Washington, Pennsylvania
    - Present day Fort Pitt (Pittsburgh) was Fort Dunmore, then Fort Duquesne and finally Fort Pitt

Acknowledgements

Thanks to my husband Dave Zwierzchowki for accompanying me on my interviews, and for the many trips to the "mountaintop" and other vantage points just to get a glimpse of this mysterious island, coming away always with the same bleak impression.

My thanks and appreciation to the Mary H. Weir Public Library and staff for holding the rich and varied history of Brown's Island in their collection, and even through the days of the COVID-19 pandemic allowed me to sift through it.

My gratitude to Pam Makricosta for her patience in reviewing my seemingly endless rewrites. Many thanks to Bob Brandt, Richard Ferguson, Mary Lynn Mitchell, Michael Runkel and John Nodianis for giving me their time and undivided attention during our interviews.

And last but not least, thanks to Jane Kraina, the lead writer of this project, for inviting me to join her on this long and somewhat rocky literary journey.

— Mary Zwierzchowski

I want to recognize an old childhood friend, Karen McClain who cheered me on during this entire process. Pam Makricosta has supported writers in this area for over fifty years and is underappreciated in this area. My husband Michael Kraina has been a loyal supporter of my writing always and has my back. I would like to thank everyone I talked to about Brown's Island. I talked to people from California, Florida, Massachusetts and Florida other states in the country. This book comes from your stories. Thanks to the *Steubenville Herald Star* and the *Weirton Daily Times* for running an article to announce the need for histories and experiences. I want to thank Dennis Jones for his support of local history and his breathtaking pictures. Dwight McUmar edited our book correcting common mistakes over and over. One of his favorite sayings is about commas, "When in doubt, leave it out." Tom Zielinsky helped me on understanding mill processes and assisted in layout. Mary Zwierzchowski has been a trooper. I know early on, she wondered, "Does Jane even have a plan? Mary loves a good mystery and I think she found some here. Also, thanks to Bob Brandt who walked in the Mary H. Weir Public about four years ago. Mary H. Weir Public Library, many, many thanks.

—**Jane Kraina**

Contents

1	THE ONE THING	1
2	PREPARING THE ISLAND TO HOUSE A COKE PLANT	17
3	THE BROTHERHOOD	24
4	THE ASBESTOS WORKERS	39
5	PIPEFITTERS AND LABORERS	46
6	THE HELPERS	55
7	THE RECORDKEEPERS	66
8	WEIRTON STEEL WORKERS	71
9	THE MAN WITH THE FLASHLIGHT	77
10	THOSE WHO DIED	88
11	AFTERMATH	107
12	A TALE FROM TWO BOBS	121
13	TRIBAL INDIANS AND EXPLORERS	131
14	WARS, ATTACKS, AND CAPTURES	138
15	LEWIS AND CLARK VISIT THE ISLAND	148
16	THE BROWNS OF BROWN'S ISLAND	157
17	THE HOOKER FAMILY	169
18	JOINED BY A MARRIAGE: THE JEWETTS AND THE STEDMANS	176
19	THE ISLAND DIVIDES COOPER, MISER AND MAGINNIS FAMILIES	185
20	MERRIMENT ON THE ISLAND AND OTHER NOTABLE EVENTS	192
21	INDUSTRIALISTS BUY THE ISLAND	202
22	RIVER OF RAMPAGE 1936	207
23	MICHAEL STARVAGGI IN PURSUIT OF THE AMERICAN DREAM	214

24 REBUILDING AND TAKEOVERS 219
25 LATER WORKERS TELL THEIR STORIES 225
26 OUTLOOK 236
An Eerie Tale of Brown's Island:
     THE UNNATURAL HISTORY OF BROWN'S ISLAND 244

Index 253

Chapter One
THE ONE THING

In the summer of 2017, Bob Brandt walks into the Mary H. Weir Public Library. He is tall and distinctive. Bob always wears a brown hat with a band. His straight posture belies the fact that he is 80. He is not the kind of figure you would forget. He has one question, "Do you have information on Brown's Island?"

"Yes, we do." I ramble over to the sturdy wooden file cabinets and pull out a manila folder with a label that says VF (for vertical file, a holder for small articles and maps and pictures). Inside this file, I know there is an article I wrote. It was the first thing I ever published and received payment in return. I could pay a utility bill or two with the money. I don't tell him about it; I figure if it has the information he needs, he will use it.

I know what is in the article. I wrote it back in the 1980s. In December of 1972, I learned my first fact about Brown's Island, a small island between the northern panhandle of West Virginia and Ohio. I knew an explosion occurred in the coke ovens being built on the island because I started dating my husband, who lived in Weirton, West Virginia in the spring of 1972. We both attended West Virginia University in Morgantown, West Virginia. My husband and his friends from Weirton discussed the explosion, the most significant accident in the steel mill's history.

Both sides of my husband's family immigrated to the United States and worked for the growing mill. My husband's dad worked there. Eventually, my husband and his brother would both join the workforce at the mill. In fact, at that time, approximately 10,000 people worked for the company. Weirton Steel Division, then part of National Steel, employed more people in the state than any other company. This distinction lasted about 35 years. Now the largest company in West Virginia is the West Virginia University Health Center.

So, in 1972, the one thing I knew about Brown's Island in West Virginia was that it was the grisly scene of an industrial accident killing nineteen men. I didn't know its size, about 3 miles, or that Native Americans had used it heavily and left artifacts giving clues to their earliest documented time on the island. I knew nothing of the grand houses built on the island or the thousands of people who picnicked on the island.

In 1972, I didn't know the island had so many perceptions: beauty, ugliness, fun, horror, romance, birth, death, ghosts, myths, and secrets. This book begins with that one thing in 1972, the most notable event on Brown's Island. Bob Brandt knew something about that one thing. He lived through the hell that occurred on December 15, 1972.

Working on the island

Robert Brandt tells his story to Mary Zwierzchowski.

Robert "Bob" Brandt worked for Weirton Steel from 1961-1986. He began working on Brown's Island in 1968. His base was a small company trailer parked across from the Ohio bridge near the north end. As a general laborer, he became familiar with all parts of the island. "The island was paradise," he said. "The south end was most beautiful, with different kinds of birds, trees, and animals. There was a soothing mist above it. No sounds of civilization, only the sounds of birds and animals of the forest."

Bob knew of the various Native American tribes that once inhabited the area and, over time, collected arrowheads and other artifacts as evidence of their existence on the island. He developed a deep respect for the tribal history of Brown's Island and an admiration for its tranquil beauty.

Then, in the spring of 1971, things began to change. Bob recalls, "That's when construction on the new coke plant got underway. Weirton Steel had contracted Koppers Company to build it. They cut down trees and slagged more than half of the island to do it." It marked the beginning of — in his words — " a paradise destroyed." They drew a line of demarcation near the south end and told us not to remove anything beyond that point." Years later, Bob learned the reason why. "Word came down from above that we were not to touch anything on the lower (south) portion of the island that might spoil the view as seen from the Williams Country Club, in Weirton, West Virginia."

On a recent visit, Bob observed the view from the clubhouse. "It still has that same pristine look about it," he said, "but what most people don't realize is that what they see from there today is less than one-third of the island. The rest of it — except for a few trees on the outer rim — is nothing more than a barren wasteland, a dumping ground, where Weirton Steel buried a lot of stuff, much of which was contaminated."

As construction at the new plant started, hundreds of skilled workers — electricians, pipefitters, welders, iron workers, and plumbers converged on the island daily. Most of them were outsourced by Weirton Steel or employed by Koppers. Bob's regular shift was eight to four. He described his morning arrival. "Every morning when I crossed the bridge from the Ohio side, I would look left and see a bald eagle perched on a tree branch near the north end. He would appear to be looking back at me, and I would get a strange tingling feeling—a premonition—like something wasn't right." The eagle thrived on carp and other fish from the river. Yet, every day it would be seen near the company trailer, preying on spiders, snakes, mice, and other critters of its liking. "We thought of him as our protector," he said.

With an uneasy feeling, Bob watched the day-by-day construction--the gradual rise of steel beams, tall stacks, and a complex pipeline network. The new state-of-the-art coke plant had become Weirton Steel's shining symbol of industrial progress. Bob viewed it differently. "It wasn't progress," he said. "It was the deliberate destruction of 100 acres of God's green earth."

In the dismal gray dawn of Friday, December 15, 1972, Bob Brandt crossed the bridge at 5:00 A.M. A light mist hung low on Brown's Island, filling the air with penetrating dampness. "The weather was not cold—just humid," he noted. "I arrived early before the big trucks started rolling in. We needed to be there to help direct them." Soon countless laborers and craftsman would follow them. News reports indicate that over 600 workers were on the island that day. Despite the high construction activity level, the bald eagle kept coming back to its resting place on the north end.

Just a few days prior, the eagle had circled the island seven times. Bob noted that the number seven in a Biblical context is a perfect number, signifying completeness.

Bob recalls the events of that morning. "Coffee break was around 9:00 A.M. They would gather in groups of three or four and share casual conversation. I was standing about twenty feet away from the ovens. A man I didn't know stood next to me, and we talked. He had just come up from the "hole" (basement of the structure). He said he was bothered by the strong smell of gas down there. He had been smelling it for several weeks and was reluctant about going back in. He also said something extraordinary. About a week prior, when he was down in the hole, he looked up and swore that he saw the image of a half-dressed Indian looking down at him. It was just a momentary thing, and then it vanished. The man knew nothing of the island's tribal history, so he didn't think much about it.

"Our coffee break was over, and the worker went back down. A short time later, the plant exploded, and the man died in the blast. I regret that I never knew his name. I tried to reach out and help, but I just couldn't. I was petrified."

Several minutes had passed. Bob turned and began walking back toward the trailer when the second blast jarred him. "I was blown face down. I received a few scratches, but mostly I was dazed. All I could see was white smoke rising from the place where the blast had occurred." His awareness of what happened came later when disturbing scenes of death and destruction began to unfold. "I couldn't believe what I was seeing," he said. "It was horrifying."

"They [Weirton Steel, division of National Steel] kept me on the island for three days. I helped barricade the bridge leading to the Ohio side. On the third day, they told me I had to bury my truck, 'because of contamination.' It was one of those trucks with a water tank. We used it to spray the roadway to keep the dust down. So, they dug this big hole, and I drove it in at a 45-degree angle. Then we covered it over. It was buried somewhere near the north end of the island, where Weirton Steel had dumped a lot of other trash in the trailer area. As far as I know, it's still there."

Still shaken from the blast's effects and the horrifying scene he had witnessed; Bob left the island that day and never returned. Nearly fifty years later, the retired steelworker remains firm in his belief that "Greed destroyed Brown's Island."

He was not the only one working on the island who talked of the former Native Americans of Brown's Island. As Mary and I started collecting data, we came across a member of the Holsinger family. Art Holsinger had a long relationship with the wondrous island turned horrible. He endured the explosion in 1972 and first encountered the island as his home in the 1930s when he was a young child.

As we began our initial research on the island by talking to people who had a connection to it, we met with Bob Brandt and Art Holsinger. They both experienced a close encounter with the blast. They talked of quite a few things: a Boys Club that held meetings and socialized on the island, chicken fights on the island, liquor from Canada dropped on the island from airplanes during the prohibition. At one time, the island got a new name, "Sin Island," Art said. "In the 1940s, circuses and carnivals drew people to the island."

Bob revealed some of his memories with Art; and we had a sense it released some of the terror he had experienced, and he began his healing journey. Bob had brought some of his artifacts, prompting Art to tell his remarkable story of the island. We continued to talk with Art, who filled in more details. Art may have been old in years, but he and his sister revealed they were still young at heart. The last time I chatted with Art, he said, "I raced down the street with my grandchildren on an electric scooter." Despite his wife's wish that he would quit working on the roof, the doctor allowed him.

The Holsinger Family Lived on the Island as Children

Art and Dorothy Holsinger tell their story to Jane Kraina.

Art Holsinger recalls his time on Brown's Island. "I lived on the island in 1934 and 1935. I was just six or seven, but I still have memories of our time on the island. Because of the Depression times, jobs were hard to come by. "Everett Ferguson offered my father a chance to be a caretaker and overseer for the island. In exchange, our family of five could live on the land for free. Art, my father, built his house on stilts because of the floods. He re-purposed wood from an old farmhouse in the middle of the island to erect our building. Our house stood by the towhead. In 1936 after we had left the island, the island flooded to the point where the waters covered everything to the trees' tops."

"After it rained, it was a good time to discover Native American artifacts. My mom and dad would go out collecting treasures almost every day. Fifteen feet of moss grew on the island, so they had to dig to unearth things. My father did find part of the airplane that crashed close to the island in 1932. "They found tomahawks, sewing needles, and warheads (pointed spears and arrows). The triangular arrowheads were for killing; when you pulled them out, they caused internal bleeding. After it rained, my parents found flints. They would glisten in the sun. On the West Virginia side, there was a beach. Unfortunately, my mother lost her Brown's Island trove of artifacts in a move."

"The other people on the island closer to the middle of the land were a group of young men who set up a "Boys Camp" of about eighty members. They built their camp on the Ohio side of the island. Members Winfield "Winnie" Scott, Marvin Needles, and Bill Robinson constructed a boat dock to access their site. A wooden sign announced its location. Bill Robinson rode around in a nice motorboat. Although they showed kindness to our family, our presence stifled some of their plans and activities.

"My mother, Iva, was a tough cookie. If she found people taking the cherries from the trees, she would get her shotgun and shoot it in the air.

"We had nut trees, cherry trees, and apple trees. Crops grew well on the island, and we kept a garden for our family to have food. Some people came over from the Toronto, Ohio, area and planted gardens. Between the natural trees on the island and the wildlife, almost everything we ate came from the island, plus fish from the river. We trapped muskrat and beaver and would sell the pelts. We ate anything that moved.

"My mother would keep us busy by making up games. One was sending us out to find nuts. Whoever found the most was the winner.

"I have to say I had a little mean streak towards my brother, Bob. Bill Robinson brought us toys, and if my brother wanted a toy, I'd throw it in the river.

"Eight swings were on the Ohio side of the island. You could swing out towards the river. Luckily, no one ever fell in the river.

"Another resident known as "the Greek" lived in a brick building towards the northern part of the island where the dike was. When the river level was down, you could walk across it. He owned a bull that roamed around. One day the bull decided to visit me in the outhouse with a curtain for privacy. Boy, did I skedaddle out of there."

"My sister Dorothy was scared at night when she took the path to the outhouse. She said, "My dad gave me a flashlight, but it wasn't enough.""

Dorothy added that 'the Greek' owned several dogs. "He was a loner. My dad would go up to see him, and he said if the dogs were there and 'the Greek' was gone, the dogs trapped him. The dogs wouldn't let him leave. It would make my dad hopping mad."

Art said, "We communicated with our relatives by whistling across the island to get their attention. To go to school, we had to take a boat. In the winter, we didn't always make it to school because of ice on the river."

Dorothy said, "My dad built me a small rowboat to get to school. I rowed over the Ohio River by myself. Our dad taught us about the weather and boating. He said the river, which he called "Old Man River," was the boss, and it would tame us, and we had to work with it. After I got to the shore, I took the streetcar to my school — Franklin School in Toronto, Ohio. On Sundays, my mom and dad would take our canoe for family rides on the river, noting the fancier boats around us.

"Even though we struggled to have enough income during the Depression years, my father always planted a big garden and would row a boat up to Toronto. Once there, he would take some of his vegetables to the soup kitchen in the town."

"I loved living on the island, and I called it the Green Jewel. It makes me sad to think of what has become of the island.

Art talked more about the island, "Hearsay was airplanes dropped whiskey on the island during prohibition. The planes supposedly came from Canada. During some of the party times, the island got named 'Sin Island.' They even had chicken fights on the island.

"My father was always trying to make extra money and went down to the Follansbee Brothers Mill to see if there was work. My father passed away in an accident on his way back from Steubenville, Ohio, on March 31, 1935. He had gone over to help his father with tasks on his land. When he returned, he saw three men trying to fix a flat tire and stopped to help. With the aid of one of the men from the broken-down car, they worked outside the vehicle when a drunk driver came and hit them where they were fixing the flat. Both my father and the other man died.

"That ended our stay and adventures on the island. My mother had to put my sister Dorothy and me in the Children's Home in the Yellow Creek area for a while. She placed my brother Bob in a foster home across the river. Later she was able to get us, and we could be together again."

"In the fifties, my wife Mathia and I had a little camp on the West Virginia Island. My wife and I boated in the carefree days of summer. You had to be careful because there was a concrete wall from the Ohio side to West Virginia. It controlled the water, and if you weren't paying attention, it would shoot your boat out. We had a good time. A treat was when Mr. Teramana brought steaks and beer for our gang of friends."

Art About the Day of the Explosion

"I worked as an electrician for the Electrical Steuben Local IBEW (International Brotherhood of Electrical Workers). Men worked in crews of ten men. One of my good friends was Jim Sommers, brother to Lou Sommers, who perished in the explosion's debris. I headed up the stairs towards the charging crane when the first explosion occurred. Jim and I worked on the coal car. I went down toward the reversing room to investigate when the second explosion hit the area. Being close to the site of the reversing room caused me to lose my hearing.

Lou had gone into the reversing room to look over a chart. As we passed through, we noticed a jammed needle with its end pointing to the top.

My understanding of the reason the blast occurred had to do with the gasholder. Pressure built up, and the surge blew the water valve. Of the many companies involved in the explosion, Weirton Steel seemed to get away with the least punishment.

The explosion's force blew up huge Hobert and Lincoln welding machines underneath the reversing room into the ceiling. One labor boss named Bill had them turn the gas lines on. This decision proved an excellent choice. If they hadn't done that, things would have been a lot worse.

We got reprimanded for taking pictures after the explosion. OSHA (Occupational Safety and Health Administration) tightened up regulations after the explosion, and our bosses yelled at us for offenses like having paint on our ladders. The experience traumatized me. We returned to the island in the evening to dig the men out of the rubble.

I did lose hearing on my right side because of damage during the accident. I never filed a lawsuit. I feel like the island will never return to its full glory. I would like to see people enjoy its natural wonders again.

Another worker on the island in the early preparation of the island witnessed a remarkable scene. Jim Black, son of Clarence Black, tells his father's story.

"An Unusual Visitor Comes to the Island"

Jim Black tells his story to Jane Kraina.

"My father, Clarence Black, worked for Weirton Steel Company as a carpenter when they began preparing the land for coke battery construction. The men cleared the ground by driving the giant excavators with a dump bed and a pan that dropped down and retrieved the dirt.

My dad said a Shawnee graveyard existed on the island, and Weirton Steel knew it. Before they built the ovens, a member of a current tribe from out of the area came to the island and told the management they would be desecrating the ancestral graves by building the coke ovens on the island. The men in charge replied that they had not hit any human bones yet.

"It doesn't matter. You have already disrespected our sacred grounds." This person, a medicine man, threatened, "Your island is cursed and will never stand. Your coke will never be good."

"My dad and others preparing the island found all kinds of Native American artifacts. They found tomahawks, hatchets, and arrowheads. My dad donated some of his items to the Wellsville River Museum, Wellsville, Ohio, including a box of arrowheads and a tomahawk."

"My father worked on the island on the day of the explosion. One of our neighbors perished in the incident. My dad went to Weirton General Hospital to help identify his body. His name was Dick Arthurs, and he was one of the electricians that died on the island. He always carried butterscotch candy and a cigarette lighter, and from those items, my father knew it was our neighbor.

"My father told me that Thomas Milsop (former president of Weirton Steel and the Mayor of Weirton) had workers cut down the apple trees on the island. Mr. Milsop enjoyed the aroma of applewood burning in his furnace."

"I also worked for Weirton Steel and showered on the island the last twenty years I worked for Weirton Steel, usually between eleven and midnight. It had an eerie quality then, especially when I thought about all that happened on the island. Under the smaller bridge located on the Ohio side, deadly water moccasins congregated."

Notes about graves of Native Americans

The Historic Preservation Act of 1966 was a federal law that sought to protect sites of historical significance. This led to each state developing a Historic Preservation agency in the 70s. The Native American Graves Protection and Repatriation Act was enacted in 1996. as evidenced below in the West Virginia Code.

According to the WV agency, their officials do not issue many permits, because most of the construction sites deal with federal agencies when beginning excavation of land.

Note: From the West Virginia Code

No person may excavate, remove, destroy, or otherwise disturb any historic or prehistoric ruins, burial grounds, archaeological site, or human skeletal remains, unmarked grave, grave artifact or grave marker of historical significance unless such person has a valid permit issued to him or her by the Director of the Historic Preservation Section: Provided, That the supervising archaeologist of an archaeological investigation being undertaken in compliance with the federal Archaeological Resources Protection Act (Public Law 96-95 at 16 USC 470(aa)) and regulations promulgated thereunder is not required to obtain such permit, but shall notify the Director of the Historic Preservation Section that such investigation is being undertaken and file reports as are required of persons issued a permit under this section: Provided, however, That projects being undertaken in compliance with section 106 of the National Historic Preservation Act of 1966, as amended, or subsection (a), section five of this article is not required to obtain such permit for excavation, removal, destruction or disturbance of historic or prehistoric ruins or archaeological sites.

In Addition (d) Notification of discovery of human skeletal remains in unmarked locations.

Upon the discovery of human skeletal remains, grave artifact or grave marker in an unmarked grave on any publicly or privately owned property, the person making such discovery shall immediately cease any activity which may cause further disturbance, make a reasonable effort to protect the area from further disturbance and notify the county sheriff within forty-eight hours of the discovery and its location. If the human remains, grave artifact or grave marker appear to be from an unmarked grave, the sheriff shall promptly, and prior to any further disturbance or removal of the remains, notify the Director of the Historic Preservation Section. The director shall cause an on-site inspection of the disturbance to be made to determine the potential for archaeological significance of the site: Provided, That when the discovery is made by an archaeological investigation permitted under state or federal law, the supervising archaeologist shall notify the Director of the Historic Preservation directly.

The One Thing

Bob Brandt points to the sign he painted while prepping the island. It was one of about a dozen items left on the island visible on December 7, 2017. Photo taken by Dennis Jones

Questions

The stories of these three men bring up several issues. Was there a Shawnee graveyard on the island, or was it just a myth? Did the 57,000 tons of slag dumped to even the ground in the middle of the island bury any secrets?

If Art had lived on the island, how many others took up residence on the island? Had anybody else perished on or about the island before the deadly explosion? We will address these questions later in our story. We continue with preparation for the building of the new coke and personal accounts of those who worked on the island in 1972

Aerial photo of island taken in 2001. Although the coke production had stopped, the site was not deconstructed until 2004. Photo taken by Jim Wark.

Chapter Two

PREPARING THE ISLAND TO HOUSE A COKE PLANT

Weirton Steel was formed in 1909 and became part of National Steel in 1929. E.T. Weir founded Phillips Sheet & Tin Plate in Clarksburg, West Virginia, with J.A. Phillips. After Phillips passed away, Weir moved the company north of Holliday's Cove, West Virginia. He provided services to the community, which came to be called Weirton after E.T. Weir. Weirton remained unincorporated until 1947. Weirton Steel consistently grew with boom times during World War II until the early 1960s. The company rose to international status as the top producer of tin plate. Steelworkers in Weirton became part of the Independent Steelworkers Union (ISU) in 1950. In May of 1957, National Steel purchased Browns Island from Mike Starvaggi for $42,000. At the time, National Steel did not have definite plans for the island but recognized its potential for expansion. According to an article published in the *Steubenville Herald-Star*, steel executives considered using it for an electric power center and warehouse storage.

By 1970, Weirton Steel employed about 12,000 people. Workers of Weirton Steel not only lived in West Virginia but also traveled from bordering states Ohio and Pennsylvania. The mills around the Ohio Valley attracted immigrants from many nations because of the high-paying jobs. Some Europeans bought into the myth that the streets of America were paved with gold. Instead, arrivals found dirt streets and row houses.

Weirton Steel Division, headed by J.G. Redline, announced plans for constructing a modern coke plant on Brown's Island. The land around the present coke plant sat next to private dwellings. Land close to the present mill in the area consisted of mountainous terrain or was unsuitable for transportation. The mill would phase out 294 coke ovens in current use on the mainland. This older equipment was now 14 to 28 years old, and its inefficiency was causing a loss in production. The existing ovens produced 4,467 tons of coke a day. Mill workers and contracted labors would build 87 new ovens with the latest technology.

In a *Steubenville Herald-Star* article, August 7, 1970, Mr. Redline said, "Of critical importance is the fact that construction of a new plant on the island will liberate a mill site which can be utilized in the future for possible expansion of facilities, such as iron-making capacity, so as to remain in a strong competitive position." This new plant would include improvements to environmental control relating to air and water quality. It would also produce coke gas to supply to the boiler house in North Weirton by converting the coal-fired boilers to gas.

Redline said site clearance had already started. Part of the preparation included raising the ground level. This process involved moving 57,000 tons of slag from the company stockpiles to the island to make the site above pool level and prevent flooding.

Roads would need clearing for transporting materials and vehicle usage. The company would add to the existing bridge from the West Virginia side, 1100 feet with pipelines, walkways, and a two-lane roadway. Another project would be to construct

Preparing the Island to House a Coke Plant

a temporary bridge from the Ohio side of the river. He said the anticipated completion time would be two years.

The new ovens featured a new design. They introduced a "slot" oven, which was twenty feet long and narrow. They stood side-by-side in groups of thirty or more. Each group constituted a battery. The process of making steel required coal. Even as technology advanced, a large majority of steel plants still used coal. The coal necessary for steel production is metallurgical coal or coking coal.

The coking coal went through a process to become coke usable for the blast furnaces. Impurities (such as sulfur and phosphorous) had to be removed. The coal was dumped in the tightly sealed oven so that air could not enter the oven and burn the coal. The ovens baked the coal to a temperature as high as twenty-one hundred degrees. They cooked for about 18 hours. A ton of coal yielded tar, ammonia, light oil, coke (¾ of a ton), and wastewater. Blast furnaces used coke for fuel. Industries purchased other chemicals to add to printing inks, solvents, dyes, and synthetic fibers. The gases from this process created useful byproducts. The byproducts plant removed materials from the gas stream. In addition to ammonia, hydrogen sulfide was produced and converted to common sulfur. Each day, the conversion unit delivered 17 tons.

In the *Weirton Steel Bulletin*, July-August 1972 edition, the publication writers described the coking procedures further, "Coal is charged through small openings in the top of the ovens by means of a hopper or 'larry' car that travels on tracks located on the top of each battery. When the coking process is complete, the doors forming each end of the oven are removed and a pushing machine, acting like a powerful ram or piston, pushes the incandescent coke into a quench car. The quench car is moved to a quench station where the white-hot coke is drenched with water sprays. When cooled, the coke becomes a grayish black, very porous fuel. It contains a high percentage of carbon and produces intense heat when used as a fuel in the blast furnaces, which produce iron for basic oxygen furnaces. This pushing and quenching system was jointly developed by Weirton Steel and Koppers." Note: Larry cars were formerly known as lorrie cars.

Many of the processes that Weirton Steel performed were already in place. Emission handling and pollution control provided significant innovation. The coal loading and heating production that were currently in use in the coke ovens on the mainland proved problematic by creating unsafe gases released into the air.

The newer technology would provide an environment within the ovens to keep the smoke and gases contained. The cost of this technology's investment would expend twenty percent of monies designated to build the new coke ovens. The contractors would supply the labor for the construction of the new coke plant.

Flood of 1972

The flood of the Ohio River on June 24, 1972 caused Weirton Steel employees to keep a watchful eye on the river's threat to Brown's Island. The river overflowed its banks and low lying areas suffered. It was the worst flood in thirty years, and it came at an unusual time. Most floods in the upper Ohio River Valley occur between January and April from snow melt and heavy rain. June that year was plagued by cool temperatures, gray skies, and an inordinate amount of rainfall.

Adding to the wet gloomy mix was yet another unusual weather system, which began in Florida on June 20. This first hurricane of the season was named Hurricane Agnes. The erratic storm battered up the eastern seaboard toward New York City and then changed course, bringing strong winds and torrential rain inland over Pennsylvania. By June 23, high water had reached the Point at Pittsburgh, where the Allegheny and Monongahela rivers meet to form the Ohio.

The swollen Ohio moved swiftly toward Chester, West Virginia, bringing misery and ruin to nearly every low-lying community from New Cumberland to Wheeling and was equally destructive along the Ohio shore. On Brown's Island, officials waited to see if their preventive measures put in place in 1971, would hold against the swirling torrents of ever rising water.

On June 24, the New Cumberland Locks and Dams recorded a crest of 45.5 feet, eight feet above flood stage. Despite the onrush of raging floodwater, the island held its ground against the remnants of Hurricane Agnes. The writers of the *Weirton Steel Bulletin* explained. "About 57,000 tons of slag from company stockpiles were used as fill on the island for plant construction. The area is 685 ft. elevation, and out of flood range. The only flooding that occurred was on the northern and southern ends and did not affect the coke plant.

Bridge leading to Ohio. The Flood of 72 covered the bridge. Photo taken by Harry Porter.

Most vulnerable was the temporary "Back River Bridge" linking the island to the Ohio shore. Water had crept up to the flooring of the one lane bridge. According to the Bulletin, some thirty-five steel slabs were placed on the 935-foot span to help stabilize it against the swift-moving back channel current.

During the 72-hour flood watch, Weirton Steel remained operational. Work continued on the new coke plant facility without incident until mid-December 1972, when a tremendous explosion rocked the island to its core.

Preparing the Island to House a Coke Plant

Bridge to Ohio in December 2017. Photo by Dennis Jones

Chapter Three

THE BROTHERHOOD

Getting ready for production required the help of many contractors. The main contractor was Koppers Company, with corporate headquarters east of Weirton in Pittsburgh, Pennsylvania. The Koppers Company built coke ovens, one of their best-selling products, and Weirton Steel paid for their services to construct the coke ovens on Brown's Island.

By October of 1971, Koppers and other contractors had completed forty percent of the work necessary to start the production of the coke ovens. At that time, they employed 350 men to work on the island. Allied Structural Steel Company of Indiana worked on the main channel bridge along the east side, linking the island to Weirton Steel Property in West Virginia. Their crew numbered thirty. Yobe and Bowers companies in Steubenville, Ohio also assisted with the project.

Local unions supplied other qualified tradespeople to prepare the island and advance the multiple structures producing coke and processing by-products. Many of the brotherhoods had their union halls in Ohio. Some of these unions included the International Brotherhood of Electrical Workers or IBEW Local 246, the Plumbers and Pipefitters 490, the Laborers Local 809, the Bricklayers Union, the Carpenters Union, the International Operating Engineers out of Wheeling, the Asbestos Union #2 of Pittsburgh, Pennsylvania, the Teamsters Union, and the Millwrights. In many ways, the story of the building of the coke plant on Brown's Island comes from the various unions' hard workers, and it was to the members of these unions that the brunt of the upcoming explosions delivered its blows.

In a *Weirton Daily Times* article in September of 1972, a reporter wrote that seasoned steelworkers were quite impressed with the new advances. They had seen the advent of the Basic Oxygen Plant, where iron mixed with steel scrap and flux made liquid steel. Now engineers showed excitement as the project neared completion. They knew that other steel producers watched the project and would imitate their improvements. Little did they know that the project would face a terrible accident and a roadblock to opening the plant on time before the end of the year.

The first explosion rocking the island on December 15, 1972, began at around 9:45 in the morning. This blast caused the most devastation. Two more explosions followed at approximately one-half hour and one hour later. The ovens were under heat treatment in preparation for a startup of the plant in late December. The men reported the smell of gas in the area to David Van Sickle, the safety manager at Koppers. Only 23 years old, he perished as he ran to see what was going on.

He became one of the 19 men who lost their lives in the accident. Ten other men suffered injuries, including one trapped inside. His story comes later. At the time of the explosion, over 670 men worked on the island. Many of those employees were taking their coffee break, which luckily reduced the number of fatalities. According to Koppers, no "special" project was going on at the blast site in the battery's extreme northeastern end. The falling debris trapped men in the basement of the structure, and gas fumes overcame them.

In a later chapter, the possible reasons for the explosion will be listed. In ensuing chapters, men and women will relate first-hand accounts of those who worked on the island.

The Electricians

The IBEW 246 provided a group of men on the island. In 1891, NBEW or the National Brotherhood of Electrical Workers formed. At a national convention held in Pittsburgh, the members changed the name to the International Brotherhood of Electrical Workers.

In the early 1940s, the union began offering courses and, in later years, apprenticeships. Their peak year of membership was 1972, the year of the accident. One million workers had joined the brotherhood of electricians that year.

Following are the stories of electricians who remembered their time on the island and their experiences during the explosion. Two union groups lost the most men. The first was the electricians (IBEW 246) and the second was the asbestos workers (Asbestos #2) from Pittsburgh. Six men died from each of their ranks.

Tragedy Hits Home

Contributed by Glen Brady from union publication

It was December 15, 1972. A large project on Brown's Island had just gotten underway, and 246 (Union #) and other workers were on the scene ensuring the proper construction of coke batteries, in addition to monitoring other projects. Water seals were in place on the batteries to ensure a steady, consistent supply of coke gas. One of the water seals — similar to a pressure valve — was defective and leaking, which created a pocket of coke gas on the job site. From out of nowhere, an unknown spark flared up, and an incredible, earth-shaking explosion ensued.

Glen Brady, II recalled the Browns Island accident, having been on the scene. "Recalling that December morning, right after coffee break, I was on top of the coke battery talking to an old friend, Barney Hanlin, when from under the coke battery, someone ran out yelling 'gas leak'.'

"Suddenly a tremendous explosion occurred right under our feet. My feet were stinging, and I was wondering which way to go. I knew I wanted off the top of the battery. I ran south the length of the battery and down the steps to the ground. I went to the area where my dad was working, and he was all right. Then, seeing workers I knew, I went to a payphone and gave names of people I saw and helped call their homes and tell their families they were okay.

"Seeing the devastation, I instantly knew people were killed or injured. Seeing the frightened look on men's faces looking for sons and friends, I can relate to 9/11 better. Elmer and Mickey knew they had to take charge and get their people to a staging area for a headcount," recounted Brady.

One man on the scene recalled how, in an instant, his world "changed from day to night." Amidst the chaos and devastation, site superintendents struggled to remain calm and immediately launched rescue efforts amidst the smoke, sirens, and tears.

Chillingly, Brady came extremely close to losing his own life that day. "Lou Sommers and Jim Brown were on their way to the battery instead." The memory will haunt Brady as long as he lives. "I can't drive by Brown's Island and not think of that day. The battery is both a powerful memorial as well as a ghost town."

In the end, nineteen men lost their lives that cold winter day; five were 246 (union number) members. Many 246 members struggled with and continue to wrestle with their question, "Why not me?" 246 member Raymond Lash wrote a moving tribute to the fallen men that day, which was published in the Local Lines.

"To all the families who have lost loved ones who were members of this local, we'd like you to know that those persons aren't forgotten, whether it be in some form of help that can be rendered to the families of these individuals or just sometimes sitting alone with tears in our eyes remembering these people. We pray that someway the loss of these fellow Brothers will draw us closer together, not just as a union, but as human beings."

Day after Accident Was Hard for Me

Jim Cunningham tells his story to Jane Kraina.

"I worked for Yobe Company, Member of IBEW-246. I went to my job on the morning of December 15, 1972. I remembered the weather was okay. I worked on the South End of the island in a building called the breaker house. It was part of the conveyor system for the coal. It was in the front section to the side and sat on the high side of the access road.

"As we were running conduit, at around 10 A.M., it felt like something struck the building. I could feel the building shake. I ran outside to see what was going on. Another explosion hit.

"I was anxious to locate my father-in-law, who was working in the silo where the explosion occurred. The amount of fire coming out of the Electrical Control Room was as wide as the access road. It wasn't a constant flame. The sight shocked me."

The general foreman yelled, "Come with me!"

"I followed him to the electrical phone room to shut off controls. I spent until lunchtime in the building. I walked to the north end, where my father-in-law had left the building five minutes before the explosion. The force of the blast lifted the first floor up from the Ground Level.

"The basement ran underneath the battery. Six of our electricians perished in the explosion. It was pandemonium. I heard the problem was in the reversing room area where gas from the mainland was feeding the new batteries. My understanding at the time was that the water seal that was supposed to protect the gas from leaking had failed."

"I returned home the night of the accident. The next day proved worse for me than the day of the incident. Most of the electricians came back on-site and worked toward shutting down the ancillary facilities in the area that produced by-products."

"In the silo area that took the brunt of the explosion, six bodies lay ready for identification. They were in a big hole. Overseers called in recovery experts. I remember one man being identified by a flap for a chain on his pocket that his wife had sewed on so that he wouldn't lose his wallet."

"It was a horrifying experience that second day. Some of my co-workers would not return to work for industrial sites, one of them being Jim Sommers, brother of Louis Sommers, who lost his life in the accident."

The Gray Dust

Richard Ferguson tells his story to Mary Zwierzchowski.

Friday, December 15, 1972, held the promise of a good day for twenty-five-year-old Richard Ferguson of Wellsburg, West Virginia. After four years of training as an apprentice, this would be his first day on the job as a certified Journeyman Electrician. Proud of his accomplishment, he was a member of IBEW Local 246 and employed by Yobe Electric.

Ferguson left home early that morning, around 6:15, and headed north on Route 2. He stopped along the way to pick up another crew member, Robert "Kenny" Gaines, both assigned to the same construction site—the new Weirton Steel coke-making plant on Brown's Island. "Outside contractors were not permitted to access the plant from the West Virginia side of the company," he explained. "So we had to cross the Market Street Bridge and go up the Ohio side on Route 7." They traveled north about four miles to Costonia, Ohio, then crossed back on the Weirton Steel temporary bridge into the cold mist of Brown's Island.

"Mornings were like that—misty and cool," he noted. "Our shift began at seven 7:00 A.M. We entered the plant from the north end and took the stairway to get up top to our work station, where we had been working on a "larry" car (a hopper car that traveled on tracks located on the top of each battery). We were getting it ready and had almost finished.

"Coffee break was around 9:00 A.M. We never left the work area. There were about eight of us. We found a place to sit on wooden benches in the electric control room. As an apprentice, I would always get coffee for the gang, but not today. I told them I was a journeyman, too. They coaxed me into going one more time. When I took a little longer than usual getting back, they razzed me about it. We were nearly always in a light, jovial mood."

Less than halfway through the break, Ferguson was reading a paper when the unthinkable happened. "First came a hissing sound," he said, "followed by a roar and then BOOM! It jolted the car we were sitting in off its tracks. My head jerked forward, and hit a cabinet. At first, we didn't know what happened, but we knew we had to get out quickly. One guy in our group started to panic. He kept yelling, 'We're going to die!' We had to calm him down as we hurried to find a way out. His reaction likely was caused by his PTSD war experience in Vietnam.

"The explosion happened in the basement directly below us. The elevator shaft was gone. We had to find another way out. We didn't know which way to run, but my instinct told me to go south. We all ran as fast as we could toward the south end, still afraid that there would be a chain reaction down the line. It was hard running through the charger lids (on top of the ovens) . The lids did not blow off, but they did create an obstacle for us in our rush to escape." They found the stairway down and safely went out to ground level where the nightmarish ordeal continued.

"I saw a man who was injured coming up from the basement. He was staggering and covered with gray ash-like concrete dust. He was bleeding from his eyes and ears. I carried him on my shoulder, but I couldn't understand why my legs were so weak. I could hardly feel them. Just then, an ambulance driver came by and told me to let go, and he would take care of him. After I put him down, I realized why I felt so weak. The man I had carried was 6' 4" and weighed 250 pounds. I saw him only once after that, but I don't recall his name.

"My first thought was to find my father and two brothers, who also were working at the plant. I walked up toward the north end and was relieved to find they were all okay. The first body I saw was that of a man wearing a red and blue checkered shirt similar to a hunting jacket. He was covered with gray dust."

Other first-hand accounts reaffirm the tremendous force of the blast. Paul Shaffer, who worked on the rigging gang for Weirton Steel, said he saw the body of a man wrapped around a pole; the explosion blew him inside-out. The force blew another victim through a chain-link fence. An unnamed observer described the horrific scene as "a brutal assault on humanity."

"We were told to report to our trailer and sign in," continued Ferguson. "That's when I realized that Kenny Gaines and several others from our crew were missing. I went looking for them but could not get near the explosion site. The devastation and the carnage-were awful. Later they asked for volunteers to help recover those still missing, and I volunteered. But several guys couldn't handle it, and they went home." Ferguson was a constable and believed that his law enforcement training gave him the ability to face the gruesome task he was about to encounter.

He described the scene. "They brought in a Bobcat and Cherry-picker machine to move the slabs of concrete and beams. We gathered the body parts and placed them with care in a large basket. The basement was about 20 feet deep. The concrete floor had blown up to the ceiling, trapping several victims. That's where we found Gaines. Gray dust covered all the men. They had been crushed beyond recognition. Gaines's face was smashed. Still, I knew who he was. He was the last one to be recovered. Some were identified by the clothes they wore."

Ferguson was humbled by what he saw and felt a sense of reverence in handling the bodies and in a gentle, respectful manner. "I just wanted to get them out," he said. "By the end of the day, we had recovered everyone who was missing identifying all but one of the victims. The bodies were transferred to Weirton General Hospital."

It was near dark when Ferguson finally left the island and headed for home. The promise of a good day had vanished into the gray dust of an unspeakable tragedy.

The young journeyman attended six funerals that week. Of the nineteen men killed in the explosion, five were members of IBEW Local 246. They were Edward Arthurs, Howard Bray, James Brown, Robert Gaines, and Louis Sommers. "I knew them well," said Ferguson. "They were my friends."

Ferguson returned to work the following Monday. He completed the Brown's Island project and then moved on. He retired from his journeyman career in 2004 and resumed his work in law enforcement, serving as sheriff of Brooke County and Wellsburg Chief of Police.

He had little knowledge of what caused the accident. "I just know that a surge of gas from the mainland had accumulated in the basement, and something sparked it. Who had actually 'kicked the lantern over' is anyone's guess. It could have been a spark from a welding torch. Then there was talk about some sort of 'curse' based on ancient Indian lore. No one really knows what happened." The specific cause of the accident remains a mystery.

In the years that followed, Ferguson never again spoke of his harrowing ordeal, and when the anniversary date — December 15-- came around, he took no note of it. "It was just another day," he said.

Nearly fifty years after the accident, the retired journeyman was asked to recall his Brown's Island experience for a book project. Surprised by the renewed interest in such a long-forgotten event, he paused for a moment then answered. "It is an important story," he said, "and it deserves to be told again."

The Secret Photographer

Harry Porter tells his story to Jane Kraina

"In 1963, I headed to Vietnam, where I served in the US Marine Corps as an electronic technician for aircraft. I enlisted at age 19, thinking I wanted to be a hero until the fear came. I did what they told me because it was crucial to follow orders. During that time, the combat wasn't severe. I did get shot at a few times, but out of the five hundred Marines I was with, only three people died due to a helicopter crash early on.

"After I came home, I worked as a white ticket electrician helper making $3 an hour with the electricians constructing Unit #1 at the Cardinal Plant in Brilliant, OH. Later I went through a 4-year apprenticeship to become a journeyman electrician. I was an electrician in the IBEW Local Union 246 in Steubenville, Ohio."

"On Browns Island, I worked on the pusher machine, a huge ram three feet wide and twenty feet high. It traveled on tracks in front of the battery, moving from oven to oven to push the coke out of the other side and into a car. In turn, the car hauled it to a quenching station where water was sprayed on it to cool it down. I ran the pusher machine during construction, and when something electrical went wrong, I had to fix it. Once while working on the device, I got trapped in front of it, and when it started moving before I was ready, I almost got smashed.

"The things I saw on Brown's Island during the explosion and shortly after proved worse than anything I saw in Vietnam and reminded me of a war zone. The fire, the sound, and the smell were horrific."

"On December 15, I was late going to my coffee break because I was working with an engineer checking out the pusher machine, and we were working on a problem that we had to finish before we could stop. That may have saved my life. The crew I was working with had coffee in the 'larry' car on top of the battery. I was starting my coffee break when the explosion happened. Because I was late for my break, I missed heading down the steps with the men who found themselves in the middle of the explosion."

"My brother-in-law Glenn Smith also would have been in danger, but Jack McCloy wanted to finish fabricating brackets. So Glenn and Jack moved away from the room used for fabricating on the battery where six electricians were killed. The 'larry' car on top of the battery served as my morning break location. The explosion hit while I was drinking my coffee there. Every floor disintegrated below my location."

"I put on my hard hat, tightened my collar, and entered self-preservation mode. I ran through the flames about 100 yards, the length of the battery roof. I was in pretty good shape back then. I called out to people as I ran to tell them to get out of there. I sprinted to the back steps to get out. I was frightened, not knowing what was happening. Unconscious men lay on the ground, outside around the battery."

"I can think of several heroes from that time that didn't get full acknowledgment. Bill Kliner pulled one man out and rushed in to get another. One bricklayer risked his life by running through the furnace and telling men to leave. He came out of the rubble; his face was white with red splotches."

"They did roll calls after the explosion to determine who was missing. They called out the names of all the crafts: the iron workers, the boilermakers, the pipefitters, the electricians, and so on."

"After the accident, I did something I wasn't supposed to do. I took pictures of the wreckage. I had to be stealthy, and I hid my camera in my coat. I had difficulty obtaining the view I wanted because I couldn't take a chance on using a flash attachment. I shot the pictures with a Minolta Single Lens Reflex, a good camera at the time. I ended up having eighty photos. I took the black and white ones at 1/15th of a second to compensate for working in the darkness. I had eighty copies made. I sold them to men who showed interest in them, and they paid me the cost of the film. "I had nightmares for years after the accident. The dream involved my son lying in his crib and getting smashed. We never got any counseling after the event."

Area before explosion. Photo by Harry Porter

"I witnessed other horrible scenes at industrial sites. I worked at the Cardinal Plant in Brilliant, Ohio, when three men got killed and others injured. While working for an outside contractor on the continuous caster in Weirton, West Virginia, a man fell near me, cutting off his arm and hitting his head. The paramedics worked hard to keep him alive but to no avail. Unfortunately, he didn't survive."

"The weekend following the Cardinal Plant tragedy, I was driving to Charleston, West Virginia, when two young guys on a motorcycle hit a car head-on and were killed. The above events happened close to the Weirton Steel explosion and affected me."

"Construction work is dangerous work. So many things can go wrong. It is hard going out there every day, knowing something can happen to you."

Parking in front of the battery. Photo by Harry Porter

Another Union Losing Six Men

The electrical workers were not the only group that lost six of their own. The Asbestos Union #2 also endured a loss of six workers. The electrical workers came mostly from Ohio, while the asbestos workers hailed from Pennsylvania.

So many of those who worked on the island had other family members on the island as well. For those waiting for news, the agony was often doubled and tripled.

A work site before the explosion. Photo by Harry Porter.

Chapter Four

THE ASBESTOS WORKERS

The Asbestos Local Workers 2 was formed in 1904. The organization chose the formal name of The National Association of Heat, Frost and General Insulators and Asbestos Workers of America. As other countries desired to join the union, the National became International. Also, as asbestos dust proved harmful to public health, it fell out of favor in industrial use. In 1972, however, the workers on Brown's Island placed it in the buildings for insulation. The union removed the word "Asbestos" from the association's title, and Asbestos Local Workers 2 became Insulators Local No. 2.

Rick Suchma
A Day I Will Never Forget

Rick Suchma shared his memories and thoughts of that day in the Asbestos 2 newsletter

"I woke up that day, and it was miserable, a lousy December day…gray, drizzling, cold and wet. Ten days until Christmas. We were working at Brown's Island, a brand new coke battery [in] the Ohio River Valley. December 15th became a day I will never forget. That was the day Local 2 and its families and friends lost six very good men. Al and Jim Tuttle were 'up-in-the-air' guys. The higher

Secrets in the Mist

and more dangerous it was, the better they liked it. Bosun's chairs [a seat consisting of rope and board that can be used to work up in the air], whatever, they were good at it. Gabby Ober (Russ) was their ground man. He could read their minds, knew what they wanted as soon as they wanted it. Gabby always talked around a Parodi cigar stub, even with a chew in his mouth. 'Hey, kid, how ya doin?' he'd ask.

"Mike Repko took a lot of pride in his work and always seemed supremely confident in his ability. Everyone liked and respected him. I didn't know Mike well but knew his nephew from grade school. Then there was Paul Byrne and Mike Crowley. I knew them best because they were 'cubs' and hung out at the bar after union meetings. You knew they were close friends because they were always bickering. If someone butted in, they'd tell him to mind his own f*****g business and then pick up right where they left off. The job was outside, so on rain days, we would work under cover wherever we could. It was a big crew, and Marty and the foreman scrambled to make sure no one lost a day. He was a class act. These were the days when the foreman, not the office, ran the job. What he said went. Period.

"Our guys and some other crafts were working around the burner boxes at the end of the battery. I'd been moved because Paul came in late, and he was usually the helper in that area. Marty had moved me to the back of the battery to help four other guys line a coke transfer car with kaowool. It was nasty work, but it was dry. Break was at 9:30. When coffee came, we climbed out on to the walkway. I looked down the battery and saw a cement block room about 50 yards away that I knew had a space heater. I said, 'It's warm. Let's take our break there.' But one of the guys--another Marty, Marty Stanton-- said, 'Let's just go into the pusher car cabin. It's closer.' So we did. It had a large window that overlooked the walkway.

"At twenty to ten, the cabin started to rock, and we heard a loud *Whuuump*. It wasn't so much an explosion as it was a large volume of air being pushed out of the way. My ears popped. We jumped up and saw an immense fireball shooting out of the breezeway at the end of the battery. We took the winding stairway from the cabin four or five steps at a time and landed running toward the river away from the battery. We didn't know if the explosions were going to stop or continue on down the battery a chamber at a time in a chain reaction. At the river bank, we looked back to see the devastation. Most of the tradesmen were gathering at the far end of the battery, so we headed there. It was total mayhem. At the front of the battery, the main steam pipe had ruptured, blowing clouds of steam into the area. The hot rail that powered the pusher car was twisted and bent, showering sparks everywhere. Buckled concrete and broken blocks laid in heaps.

"As we stood there in shock, Roland Kline let out a yell, 'My friends are in there!' He rushed over to a pile of rubble in the middle of the wreckage and began throwing broken block and concrete pieces out of the way. I'll never forget that. With tears in his eyes, he bellowed to us, 'Come on! We've got to find them!' That man's courage amazed me. I was twenty-two years old and scared to death.

"There was still a lot of fire, steam, and sparking going on. Another smaller explosion hit. A safety team arrived and moved us further away. They had to go back and pull Roland out, bringing him to where hundreds of us were now standing, scared and wondering who of our friends were missing.

"The safety crew spread word for us to go to our shanties and get a head count...we found out six of our own were missing, along with thirteen other craftsmen. Nineteen lives snuffed out—just like that. I later heard that the cause was a leak in the gas preheater that fed fuel to the battery. The preheater was in a basement room below the breezeway where Al, Jim, Gabby, Mike, Mike, Paul, and the other men were having coffee. The ceiling of the room was poured concrete instead of a grating, so the gas couldn't dissipate. Somehow the trapped gas ignited, causing the first explosion. A dumb design cost 19 lives. The block room where I wanted to take our break was completely gone. Nothing left at all. There are other stories about circumstances that kept guys out of that particular area that fateful day. I wish there were at least six more. Our lives are fragile. Things beyond our control can bring tragedy. Help keep the odds down and watch out for each other. We are all part of something special."

Bill Yund
Unwelcome Death

Bill Yund contributed his summary of the accident in Asbestos 2 newsletter.

"Construction is a dangerous industry, and disaster can be sudden. This is an account of one of our worst disasters, the coke oven explosion at Brown's Island in 1972, where six of our brothers lost their lives.

"There's not much coke battery work around anymore, but before the collapse of the steel industry, many insulators worked on them. The ovens heat coal at extremely high temperature to carbonize it, turning it into coke to make steel. They stink enough to make you loopy, are hot enough to burn the soles off your boots, toxic enough to make you sick, and dangerous enough to kill.

"In 1972, there was a contract to build new coke units for Weirton Steel at Brown's Island in the Ohio River near Weirton, West Virginia above Steubenville, Ohio. In December, the job had been underway for 32 months, and the plant was scheduled to begin producing a million tons of coke per year in '73. The job was behind schedule, but some of the ovens were already fired. A 36" [or 54" - reports vary] pipeline brought gas from a plant across the river. There were 676 people on the island. Many would be injured, and nineteen lost their lives. Six would be insulators. It was ten days before Christmas, and snow was falling. There was a strong smell of gas around the gas pre-heat area, and two men were overcome by fumes. An ambulance was called, and a safety man came to investigate. He wouldn't leave alive.

"9:30: coffee break. Men settled down and read the newspapers. The Steelers were coming on strong after a half-century of mediocrity. For a few more minutes, that seemed important. About 9:40, the first muffled explosion was heard, followed by a massive second explosion. A brick inspector said it 'sounded like an atomic bomb.' Already running from the growing smell of gas, he was lifted and blown about 20 feet. He survived, bleeding from the head. Two miles away in downtown Weirton, buildings shook and windows shattered.

"At the scene, steel twisted like bread sticks, concrete catwalks blew away, brick walls were destroyed, and hot electrical lines menaced survivors. Some buildings were jolted from their foundations. Most of the deceased were in a basement below the battery. Victims included Weirton Steel employees, but the majority were construction workers, including six insulators, known in those days as Asbestos Workers. Some victims were taken to a makeshift disaster center at Weirton General Hospital, others to a hospital in Steubenville. There was considerable confusion.

"The need for an accident assembly area was evident in the initial miscount of fatalities and problems identifying the missing, victims, and survivors. First reports listed 21 dead. Three insulators were named, three more listed as missing. The news media had difficulty getting information. A Pittsburgh news helicopter was denied permission to land at the site. At least one hospital posted a security guard to bar newsmen from interviewing survivors. Representatives from the general contractor said all men in the area were accounted for, and all were subcontractors. Neither statement was true. There were pronouncements concerning the costs and the need to resume operations quickly. OSHA would eventually cite Weirton Steel for failure to provide a safe work site, failure to provide adequate warning of the hazard, and for requiring workers to work in the coke oven battery basement without a safe exit. The fine was $2100.00. The insulators lost to their families were the following: James Tuttle; lbert Tuttle, age 34. Michael Repko, age 45; Michael Crowley, age 26; Paul Byrne, age 22; and Russ Ober, age 55.

"It is particularly unwelcome at the holiday time of happiness and family bonding. For the families of these men, the holidays of 1972 were tragic; each season since touched with memory and melancholy. The day was darkly marked into many lives."

Construction summer of 1972. From Weirton Steel Bulletin. Courtesy of Weirton Museum and Cultural Center.

Chapter Five

PIPEFITTERS AND LABORERS

The accounts below come from members of two more unions. The headquarters of both unions stood in Steubenville. The first two accounts are from the Pipefitter/Welder, Local Union 490 of Steubenville (as it was known in 1972). This brotherhood has since merged with 95 (a Cambridge, Ohio unit). They renumbered it 495 to reflect the change.

Founded in 1936, The Laborers Union 809 has its base in Steubenville, Ohio. It serves Jefferson, Columbiana, and Harrison Counties in Ohio and Brooke and Hancock Counties in West Virginia. This union provides workers to the *Building Trades and Heavy and Highway Contractors.*

Save the Battery

Michael Runkel tells his story to Mary Zwierzchowski.

The morning of December 15, 1972, Michael Runkel was home asleep when the call came. "It was my brother," said Runkel. He told me there had been an explosion at the coke plant on Brown's Island, and he was calling to check on me. He thought I was scheduled to work that morning, but my shift had been changed to night turn—3 to 11—just a few weeks earlier. That's when I became certified as a journeyman pipefitter/welder. Had I still been working as an apprentice, I would have been on the Island the morning of the explosion." The twenty-six-year-old journeyman was employed by Songer Company and was a member of the Plumbers and Pipefitters Union, Local 490.

That afternoon, Runkel set out from his home near Follansbee, West Virginia, and headed north on Route 2. He wondered what his job assignment would be and in what direction he should go — over the temporary bridge from the Ohio side or the Weirton Steel bridge on the West Virginia side. "I bypassed the Market Street Bridge to Ohio and headed straight to Weirton [the north end]," he explained. "I parked my car in the lot at Gate No. 1 and from there caught a ride with a mill worker who drove me across the bridge to the Island. When I got there, I could see a lot of confusion. The place was in shatters. The EMTs and firefighters were still there searching for those still missing. I saw a guy stuck on a steel beam. It looked like his body had been blown open."

"I went directly to our trailer and reported in. That was where we gathered for our assignments. I learned that one of our guys, Bill Kliner, had been killed in the blast. They said he went in [to the blast area] and pulled one man out and went back a second time to help another, and that's when he died.

"After some discussion, our general foreman decided that we would work to repair the damaged pipelines in order to save the battery. If we lost heat to the furnace and let it cool down, the battery would be ruined. The order to make the repairs came from Weirton Steel. They seemed more concerned about saving the battery than they were about saving lives.

"We accepted the assignment but were delayed until the

correct size of piping was brought in from Richmond, Ohio. I was surprised at how quickly it was delivered. There were about ten guys in our crew. We worked like dogs getting it done and had to work carefully to make sure that it was done right. It was a temporary fix, but we had to maintain heat to the furnace. There were about 30 ovens to one battery. We had to go in and make the same connections — 30 times over — to each oven."

It was a repetitive, time-consuming task, but they got the job done. They repaired the pipelines, restored heat to the furnace and, in the process, saved the battery.

It was well past midnight when the dedicated crew from Local 490 finally wrapped up the project and began leaving the Island. In the background, cleanup crews continued to work through the night, still mindful of any human fragments yet to be found among the twisted wreckage of steel and concrete.

The young journeyman pipefitter, just two weeks on the job, hitched a ride back to the mainland to Gate No. 1, where he had parked his car. On the long drive home, his thoughts drifted back to the day's events.

Runkel knew there was nothing that he and his fellow crew members could have done that would have altered the outcome of that dreadful morning. They simply completed their assignment to the satisfaction of the company, which was to save the battery.

A Day of Confusion

Robert tells his story to Jane Kraina.
(Last Name Withheld at his Request)

"I worked the daylight shift the morning of the explosion as a pipe fitter. I was 26 at the time, married with one daughter. I

Pipefitters and Laborers

had served in the Air Force in Southeast Asia and had some pipe fitting experience before that. They needed electricians more than pipefitters and transferred me to work on telephone switching.

"I believe the information that the papers reported was incorrect. The newspapers stated that not many Weirton Steelworkers were on the Island. However, as the date for starting production on the Island loomed days away, many from the Weirton division showed up to do test runs on the coke ovens. People could barely turn around in the crowd on the Island.

"The mainland's gas lines provided gas over to the Island until full processes could begin on Brown's Island. The men measured the pressure coming from the gas pipes. On the Island inside the control room, measuring devices recorded the pressure on dials. The pressure inside the gas lines swelled over the acceptable limit. According to what Koppers Company told me, a tar plug on a coke gas line caused the water seal to blow, and the seal pot released gas, causing the explosion.

"The Koppers engineer from England directed the effort to keep more explosions from occurring. He negated the idea of shutting the gas off all at once. He said the gas would follow the flame, thus traveling the line and returning to the mainland, causing a massive problem.

"Weirton Steel employees came and pulled the recording equipment on the lines out of the area, and they disappeared. I went back to work on the Island for another six months to finish the machinery's repairs.

My Relatives Suffered Injuries

Gary Ogden tells his story to Jane Kraina.

"My dad Ross Ogden, and my uncle Ted Schiffner (both from Rush Run, Ohio), worked on the Island. My brother-in-law Donald Long (from Rayland, Ohio) also had a job on the Island. They all suffered injuries in the Brown's Island explosion. My dad had broken ribs, and the force of the blast threw my uncle across the room. My brother-in-law had minor injuries and was part of the 'clean-up crew.'

"The explosion collapsed the concrete floors. Some pancaked men in between the concrete; it was a terrible explosion. Many men who belonged to the local laborers union 809 are still around; however, the old-timers who worked that day are mostly gone, including the above family members. I recall their stories of that hellish day. It helped me enforce safety rules in my later life. Some ambulance-chasing lawyers contacted my dad wanting to sue, but he declined and was just glad he had a job, as most did back then.

"Years later, from 1988-89, I worked for a Pittsburgh company. They had a warehouse on Brown's Island. We rebuilt the entire phone system for Weirton Steel, backing it up with fiber optics and microwave. I walked around the Island, found some arrowheads on the far end. I have got a friend who was a security guard at the entrance to the bridge crossing the river to Route 7."

My Father and I both Worked on the Island

Charles Long, tells his story to Jane Kraina.
Charles is the son of Donald Long above.

"My father, Donald, served as a steward for the union. He sustained minor injuries in the Brown's Island tragedy. His best

Pipefitters and Laborers

friend, Kenny Harris, general foreman, perished in the accident. The two of them were at the bottom of the steps, making rounds. My dad left to take a break, and Kenny stayed to finish rounds and was there when the blast hit. Kenny's family identified him by his belt buckle and his wallet. His wife passed away recently. She had received a settlement from Koppers.

"My dad said there was a stink from the coke flare stack. Men were bricking, and someone from the mainland shut off the gas being piped to the Island. This action caused an explosion in the basement. The blast crushed the welding machines and smashed the concrete.

"I worked on the mainland in 1979 when they planned doubling the size of the batteries. In 1980 we were putting in piers, and I worked on a cooling tower. They did not finish with the expansion because the economy took a dive.

"Someone told me one tower contained naphthalene gas. The company also had a pit and put hazardous material in it.

"Sixty people worked on the cooling towers on the Island. They had maintenance buildings and a water treatment facility on the Island. So about a hundred people worked on the Island when I was there."

Working on Brown's Island was My First Assignment from the Union

Dean Richards tells his story to Jane Kraina.

"The Laborers Local 809 served on the laborer concrete gang who employed me as an outside contractor. 809 in Steubenville, Ohio, served to assign men in the area who wanted work. I started the job on Brown's Island when I was 23 and newly married. This gig was my first assignment, beginning my association with the Laborers Union, where I continued to work for another thirty-eight years.

"My stay on the Island began in October 1970 and ended about thirty-one months later. I worked steady daylight on my job. As a part of the gang, one of our tasks involved constructing all the pads that would support the ovens.

"During construction, the contracted workers made up the majority of people on the Island. Weirton Steel also had inspectors on the Island. They proved congenial.

"The rain came down on December 15, 1972. I heard a loud explosion and then saw a huge ball of fire coming after the thunderous noise. The fireball was the size of a house. I was about a hundred yards away from the explosion. The fear I experienced stemmed from not knowing what was going on. We had no alarm system to notify us of problems. I did not get hurt in the accident. My foreman, Kenneth Harris, died in the accident. He was pleasant but also a no-nonsense kind of man.

"Our group found arrowheads on the Island. These were some of the most common items found on the Island."

My Husband Suffered Double Trouble

Christine Pearson Tells her Story to Jane Kraina.

"I married Gerald Michael Pearson on June 22, 1968. He passed away in 2002. December 15, 1972, changed our lives. Everyone called him 'Mike'. I always addressed him with the name 'Ger.' My husband served in Vietnam and witnessed a bad experience with one of the men in his platoon. After an attack, he grabbed a fellow soldier by his arm, only to discover his arm was not attached to his body.

On top of battery in October 1972. Photo by Harry Porter

"So for him, coming home, joining the IBEW 246, and being in an area close to the eventual explosion, brought up painful memories of the war. Kenny Gaines, a good friend of my husband, had become a journeyman. He was also a social friend and caught the garter at our wedding. Kenny Gaines and his girlfriend and the two of us went out together. On the day of the blast, Kenny had told Ger to go on break. Ger said the explosion was louder than anything he heard while he was in Vietnam. Kenny did not survive the fiery disaster.

"I was home the day of the explosion. Before we had kids, I had worked in the stenographic pool in the mill. We had made a decision that I would be a stay-at-home mother. Ger had gone to work early that morning for his 7 to 4 shift. I talked to a friend who asked if I had heard about the explosion when an operator broke in with an emergency call. It was my grandmother telling me to call my aunt Adeline. Her husband was Henry Paravano, a supervisor in by-products. Ger had let my grandmother know that he had seen Henry and that he was OK.

"I never worried my husband had been hurt in the accident. I believe the best until I am proven wrong, and I just thought he was coming home. I really didn't know absolutely until my husband walked through the door. He was called back to the Island to try to locate personal items.

"He never talked about the accident after that. He suffered inside and drank more afterward. So, in a way, two grisly experiences in succession slowly drained the life out of him."

Chapter Six
THE HELPERS

Some of My Memories Were Erased

Charles Fach tells his story to Jane Kraina.

"I was 22 and had just graduated as a registered nurse from Ohio Valley Hospital School of Nursing. Ambulance Service Incorporated (ASI) hired me when I was eighteen and I worked there during my nursing training. I was at home when I got a call to assist with ambulance duty. I remember driving my motorcycle to the ASI headquarters. Robert J. D'Annibale headed up ASI, and his daughter runs it now.

"My motorcycle helmet was still on my head upon my arrival to the island. It helped protect me once I started assisting the accident victims. It was the smartest thing I took with me. I wish I could recall more on Brown's Island, but the events on the island became erased from my memory right after I was there.

"Dr. Sanford Press, who worked with Big Red School in Steubenville, took charge of medical assistance. I went to the 3-11 shift at St. John's, where they treated the majority of the injured. They took the dead to the Weirton General Hospital. St John's shut down elective surgery to keep the operating rooms open in case men needed emergency surgery, but the staff at Ohio Valley did all but one of the operations.

"Those who work in the emergency rooms and out in the field as ambulance workers see many horrible injuries and violent circumstances. They suffer PTSD from viewing gruesome sights.

"I worked as a nurse for various medical facilities. I became a private pilot for twelve years. I have taught classes at Trinity and Weirton Medical Center in emergency and psychiatric care. I am now retired."

An Unforgettable Call to Our Fire Station

Alex Gryskevich III tells his story to Jane Kraina.

"I was a volunteer for the Oakland Fire Department when we got the call. I went to the station, and they asked for a relief car. My father was chief of the Oakland Fire Department, and he worked at Bowers Supply in Weirton. I rode over with another man driving my car. He stayed, and somebody took my new car back. I rode the firetruck back from the scene.

"Chief City Fireman Clyde Maze took charge of everything. We used a Stokes Basket to remove the men from the reversing room. Because of the threat of ensuing explosions, we did not begin recovery of the dead bodies until between four and eight-thirty at night. They had put ladders down in the basement. We formed a chain of men to help get the concrete out piece by piece because the concrete floor wasn't stable.

"The explosion was so forceful that seams in the men's jeans split open. They lost settings in their gold rings. The faces on their watches broke off, and all stopped at the same time.

"I heard an uncapped valve caused the problem. An eight-inch gas line delivered gas into the reversing room. At that time, the gas came from the mainland coke plant. A credible source told me they hadn't finished connecting one of the gas lines, and the gas escaped out of the open pipe. Also, I heard someone walked out with a lit cigarette. They used the elevator shaft as a makeshift lunchroom, and they took their break in there.

"I remember one of the men we brought over the wall. After the man identified his brother, his emotions got the better of him, and he started running away to go to the river.

"I was twenty years old when I helped out at Brown's Island. I didn't sleep for three nights and suffered from PTSD. In my thirties, I became friends with a psychiatrist who helped me deal with the lingering trauma. I could look at things differently and accept the inevitable.

"I am a lifetime member of the Volunteer Fire Dept. I had been laid off from the mill at Thanksgiving. I got married on February 3 and started back to the mill two days later. I worked for the Mason Gang at the BOP. After I got laid off again, I worked at the City of Weirton Fire Department for twenty-seven years and then worked as a janitor for the City Building until I turned sixty-five."

We Carefully Loaded Men into the Ambulances

Ray Pratt tells his story to Jane Kraina.

"The fire departments came from all over, including Colliers and Hooverson Heights. We could not do much until someone turned the gas off. It wasn't until later afternoon but still daylight that they could get in to remove the bodies. On both sides of the battery was a roadway.

"The volunteer firefighters lifted the men out of the rubble using a Stokes basket, a metal basket for rescue. They placed a blanket under the patient and gripped the sides of the rolled blanket to lift the men into the Stokes basket. The firemen wrapped some of the men in their clothing. To go down into the explosion area required an air pack with an air bottle. We hadn't been trained yet in medical treatment. EMTs were not part of ambulance teams or firefighters then. After the Brown's Island incident, the management made sure people had more training. I would ask the name of their coworker. Next, I would write their name on a fire extinguisher tag and tie it to the Stokes basket. We loaded one body at a time into the ambulance. The victim's coworkers would identify him. We loaded them into the ambulances, which, in my memory, was three or four.

"We stayed until they took all the bodies from the scene, about 9 o'clock. Trucks came in with food and coffee to feed us. I believe that came from the Salvation Army.

"Anytime we encountered a gas leak on the job, we would remove all the bodies from the site. Unfortunately, finding the source of the gas leak put some of our workers at risk for injury."

Nurse, Nurse, Come Quick

Jeanne Noe tells her story to Jane Kraina.

"My story of Brown's Island is highly unique as I worked as a nurse on the island, the only woman among 1500 men, other than a secretary who served on the island for a short time. I lived in Toronto, Ohio. From 1947 to 1950, I attended the Ohio Valley School of Nursing and worked at the Ohio Valley Hospital.

"My son attended high school, and I worked part-time as a

nurse at the titanium plant in the southern part of Toronto. I was golfing at the former Dyer Country Club with my friend Thelma Weymouth. She said to me, 'My husband Howard, a superintendent at Koppers on Brown's Island, needs a nurse to tend to the men who have medical needs on the Island'.

"When I asked a few of my nursing friends if they were interested, they wanted to work on the island. However, when they informed their husbands about the job opportunity, their husbands were uncomfortable with their wives working with so many men. I finally took the job. I had to wear my white uniform with white hose and shoes as that was the norm then. When I started on the island, OSHA was starting and wanting more regulations in the workplace. Weirton Steel did not require physical exams, nor did they insist on safety glasses. I treated 200 men a month with eye issues such as a cinder that ricocheted into their eyes. Some men would bring me artifacts they found on the island, primarily the heart-shaped ones.

"One task I set up while a nurse was obtaining physicals on the men. I would work through a couple of lunch hours a week to record blood pressures and check the men to determine who needed further care. An ambulance and driver were on the island each day in case of emergencies. I would do initial first aid and help the men into the ambulance provided by Ambulance Services Inc. (ASI) run by Robert D'Annibale.

"On the day of the explosion, someone came to my trailer and said, 'Nurse, nurse, come quick.' I grabbed my black bag with medical supplies and started running. David Van Sickle, the safety manager, and I tried to get in the ambulance they brought around, but it couldn't maneuver on the railroad tracks they had put down to bring the gas into the island. They hadn't laid down the dirt yet. David told me, 'You get in the ambulance, and I will meet you there'. He went on foot to the ovens.

"We had to go down the west side and around the south side to get to the coke battery area. I was heading up the north side when the place blew. Paul, the driver of the ambulance, ran toward the bridge. I said to myself, 'Dear God, help me.' I was twenty feet away from the smoke and fire.

"My safety manager, David Van Sickle, perished in the explosion. We had become close friends. I would have entered the area where the trapped men were enclosed with the ambulance workers Harvey Templin and John Bowers, but they did not have a gas mask that would fit me. I did help them load men into the ambulance. I also tended to men around the area.

"They asked me to stay on the island for a couple of days after the explosion. They put a cot in my trailer, and I spent the nights there also. I took care of 70 men after the explosion. Some just had cuts and bruises, but others suffered more severe injuries after the blast. Some men felt so spooked after the accident that they drove straight off the bridge and headed to other towns such as Cleveland. OSHA clamped down with regulations after the accident. Items such as safety glasses became mandatory.

"I attended four or five funerals after the explosion. I also visited men in the hospital. One man from Chester nicknamed 'Lucky' was outside day of the accident. He and his wife showed their gratitude for favors I had done. On the day of the explosion, he was outside saying, 'Help me, help me.'

"I hadn't recognized him because his face was black. 'Don't you know me'? he asked. 'I'm Lucky'.

"I still recall how his entire face looked 'melted'. He was in isolation with severe burns for quite a while at Ohio Valley Hospital. I visited him in the hospital.

Area outside of room where electricians were trapped.
Photo by Harry Porter

"The weather turned cold the evening of the explosion. All I had for my feet was my nursing shoes. A man went to a shoe store in Toronto and bought me a pair of high calf boots.

"I received many thanks for my job. One little girl wrote me a note expressing gratitude. She wrote, 'Thank you for saving my daddy's life'. I had administered CPR on her father. Donald Lazas (sp.?) sent a letter to the editor of the *Steubenville Herald-Star* after the accident. This thank you came from a Koppers employee from Rayland.

"Every time I read a newspaper article about the explosion on Browns' Island December 15, 1972, I am disappointed to read no words of praise for Jeanne Sunseri, RN.

"These are my own words, but every man who was working on the Island that terrible, terrible day shares my feelings that she was not a part of the rescue team; she was the rescue team.

"I first saw her seconds after the explosion. Whenever I think of that day, the first thing I see in my mind's eye is her jumping out of the ambulance while it was still moving and running into the Holocaust of smoke and fire without a moment's hesitation.

"I don't know how many men were around me, maybe fifty, but we were all rooted to the ground, and we were all watching our 'Genie' nurse rushing and running, her uniform covered with blood and mud, leading men out from the fire and smoke. I know she personally rescued five men all by herself and had the ambulance filled with men before any other rescue team came on the scene.

"All the rescue teams deserve the highest praise possible for their courage and bravery in their actions on that day.

"But being in the group of men who tried to assist the rescue teams, I know there was only confusion until our beautiful nurse, [Jeanne, Genie] decided what should be done, then put us all to work doing it.

"Somebody should ask the rescue teams about Jeanne's outstanding work actions that day. Then she would be sure to get the honors she deserves.

"She went into the building with the rescue team and was in the building when the second explosion happened, and she wasn't wearing a gas mask. That wasn't bravery? That wasn't putting her life in jeopardy to save others? That doesn't deserve praise?

"And in the early afternoon when gloom and depression were settling on all of us, when we knew the men unaccounted for would be dead, only one spark kept us there. Our beautiful nurse, Jeanne.

"She had to be a <u>Genie</u> to be everywhere at once, because I know she questioned every one of us who stayed on the Island to help, about who might be missing, and where that man would be working.

"I know she wanted rescue equipment that we couldn't get anywhere, but she appealed to all of us, to appeal to someone else to find the equipment, and we got the equipment.

"Jeanne was not just an Angel of Mercy on December 15, 1972. She was sent by God to lead us that day. No man or group of men or all the living men on the Island that day equaled one minute of the job she did that day for those living and the dead.

"Our nurse deserved written words of praise even before the explosion. I've been doing construction work for fourteen years, and when there has been a nurse on the job, she was competent. But Jeanne has qualities that most nurses lack. She has a soft touch that most construction men have never known. And she has compassion, and she is beautiful. And she has a smile that makes us forget about Florida oranges.

"I thank God for giving me a job with Koppers, and I hope Koppers thanks God for giving them Jeanne." [from] **A Koppers Employee**

"Koppers gave me a generous bonus, so I took my son to Florida for a vacation. Koppers asked me to work as a plant nurse in Follansbee from 1976 to 1977. They honored me with a plaque for my service.

"I moved to California and lived in La Jolla. My parents came to visit me there, and we had a splendid time for a couple of months. Not much later, after they returned to Toronto, they became ill. I came back to help them in their family home. After they died, I bought myself a baby blue Cadillac with powder blue seats. The model was the last of the 'big Cadillacs.' The snow that year came up to my car's windows, so my friend and I decided to go to Florida. I moved there.

"I had made up my mind to look into a job at the King's Hospital in Saudi Arabia. I would work in a compound. While I waited for the final contracts to be drawn up, my life took a dramatic turn.

"I golfed in Florida, and on the course, I met Jimmy Noe, who owned a brick construction company. He asked me to golf with him the next day. We played nine holes, and he asked for another match. We ended up married, and life was good until he passed away twelve years later.

"I have been in Florida for 37 years, and I still work as a private duty nurse. I maintained friendships I made from the Island, particularly with the Weymouths who initially told me about the job. Interestingly, in one conversation we had after the accident, he said he would rebuild the solid floors with grates. This feature would allow the gas to dissipate.

"We visited each other over the years. I still go to the country club and socialize. My son from Brion Sunseri works in Florida, heading Ad-VANCE Talent Solutions, Inc. in

"I Got a Job Offer from Weirton Steel on the Day of the Explosion

Steven Pawlock tells his story to Jane Kraina

I was a professional diver in Florida. I taught skin diving and had my own business. I dove for the FBI around the Weirton

The Helpers

area. They once had me try to find a safe that had been thrown in the river.

I dove around Brown's Island the day of the explosion. Weirton Steel offered me a job that day. I worked on the tugboats when the propellers broke. They called them screws. I also found a radio that had gone into the river.

A captain of the boat and the coordinator of construction on the Browns Island Bridge worked on putting piles or vertical supports that were hammered into the ground. These piles braced the beams for the bridge. He offered me a blank check if I could locate the piling extractor that got lost.

I had been teaching diving at Washington and Jefferson College in Washington, Pennsylvania. I got a call from Henry Tarr, assistant of the fire department. He asked me to come up to the downtown warehouse and help with the men they were trying to identify. The nurse asked me my name and when I told her she said, "They are waiting for you."

Many helpers aided rescue efforts on the day of the explosion and it was grim work. It took a lot of courage to sift through the rubble unsure of what would be found. As you will see ahead men gave up their lives in attempt to rescue their friends and coworkers.

In addition, men from the ambulance services disobeyed orders to not enter the building but they chose to retrieve men from a scene of darkness and smoke. Many people served to identify the lost on that day and even if quiet about their actions they still had to deal with haunting memories. All the people that day in the field and in the hospitals deserve thanks as we reflect on that day.

Chapter Seven

THE RECORDKEEPERS

I Signed up the New Union Workers

Micki Cline as contributed to Jane Kraina.

"My father, a crane operator, and I worked on the island the fateful day of the explosion. As usual, we drove together to work.

"I worked for Koppers Company in the payroll office located on Brown's Island. I was only eighteen when I started my job (in March or April of 1971.) I had married a few months before I began my position. My maiden name was Hervey. I stayed at my job until around July of 1973. At that time, my husband and I wished to start our family.

"The business office where I worked stood directly in front of where the explosion occurred. My office manager was a man named Foster. My days consisted of payroll duties. I signed up all the new union workers when we hired them, such as pipefitters, laborers, ironworkers, carpenters, and other skilled workers. The building of the coke batteries involved hiring only union employees.

"I was the only girl in an office with about twelve guys. At lunch, they would teach me how to play the card game euchre. After about six months, they did hire a female nurse.

"My father and I worked on the island. He was a crane operator out of the WV operating engineers union. Koppers paid his salary. My father was there a month or two before I started. I believe Koppers laid my father off around the end of 1973. We both lived in Bloomingdale, Ohio, at the time. My father would pick me up each morning, and we would drive to work together in his Volkswagen. He was a large crane operator.

"I remember that day and most of the events, but some of the names have slipped from my memory. I had no premonition of anything eventful about to happen. Right before the explosion, workers reported to our safety manager David Van Sickle that they detected a gas smell. He was in the office next to mine. It was all open area. I remember he grabbed his hard hat and rushed out the door. He perished in the intense blast. Workers identified him by his colorful socks. Sadly, he was only twenty-three, and he and his wife had just had a baby.

"From my location in my office, we did not smell the gas odor. There was an emergency siren that had a continuous ring. We did have regular emergency practices. The siren went off immediately after the explosion. I remember the men always saying if a particular siren blew and it was continuous, run out the back door and head for the river. And when that siren blew, we sped out of the back door.

"My father was operating a large crane at the scene of the explosion. It was break time, and we had just had a layoff, or there would have been more death and injury. My father stayed in his crane at break time instead of climbing down and then back up again 15 minutes later. The windows cracked in his crane, among other damage. I did not know it at the time, but the explosion force shattered his hard hat. Wearing that hat most likely saved his life.

I remember we were escorted to another building through the parking lot away from the blast area. At that time, I could see my father's crane. I did control myself but cried, knowing he could be injured or worse. About an hour later, one of the foremen brought my father to me to prove he was okay. We were the lucky ones. My brother was part of the recent layoff. If not, that would have been his work area also. Aside from that day, I greatly enjoyed my work on the island."

The Explosion Hit as I Took My Typing Test to Get Hired

Deborah (Hennis) Pollard contributed this story.

"I was twenty years old, and my friend Micki Cline had been there and knew I was looking for work; Micki got me an interview. I was familiar with the island as my family and friends had reserved spaces on the island for our boat docks and boated. We had many happy times with our friends. Since I was familiar with the area, I knew right where to go.

"There was a one-lane bridge, and I drove over that bridge just thinking about getting a new job. I was met at the end of the bridge by a very nice young man. He took me to the trailer where I needed to go for the job interview. I was welcomed and seated at a typewriter to do a typing test.

"During that time, there was a thunderous noise, and the trailer shook! I looked around to see if anyone else was alarmed by the noise and the trailer shaking. There were some serious, questioning looks on everyone's face. I turned and asked someone if this was normal, and they said no and hurried past. The next thing I knew, someone told me to get out of the trailer, and my friend came up next to me. We went out the door, and a couple of men physically picked Micki and me up (at the time, I was barely 100 pounds) and ran with us to a big building. Everyone was running, and we could hear sirens.

"At some point, the workers told us there had been an explosion. There was no access to the phones at that time. Since there was only a one-lane bridge, we couldn't get off due to the need for the ambulances and firetrucks to get on the island. We stood there, trying to comprehend what had happened. And yes, we were scared. As we were standing there, I recognized a neighbor, Ed McKenna, who came rushing over to me. I hugged him and was relieved to know he was okay. He was just as unsettled as we were, but his main concern was to ask me to let his wife know that he was okay, as I would be able to get off the island before he would, and he had no way to contact her.

"I later found out that the blast's force had killed the young man who had been my first contact. He and his wife had just had a new baby. I was devastated. Even though I had only spent a few minutes with him, his face was in my memory, and I felt the loss for his family.

"As soon as they had removed the injured, we could get to our cars and leave the island. As we left, we were pretty shaken up.

"As all of this was taking place, my mom had been grocery shopping. I learned later that as she was checking out, the cashier, a neighbor of ours, asked her how I was doing. She said that I was fine and that I had gone to a job interview that morning on Brown's Island. Then our neighbor Doris asked her if she had heard from me and mom said no. Then Doris asked her if she heard about the explosion. My mom was frantic! She rushed out of the store and got to the nearest office of a friend so that she could use the phone to call our neighbor's wife to see if she had heard from her husband, who worked on the island. Ila had not yet heard from Ed, her husband. All they could do then was to wait.

"I stopped at my mom's on my way home. Once she knew I was okay, I ran across the road to let Ila know that Ed was okay. When she opened the door, she was crying. I kept saying Ed's doing well. and she said, "how do you know?" I told her that I had talked to him, and he wanted me to let her know he was okay. She was so relieved. "I did go back and work for Koppers. I was initially going to type W-2s in my job. Instead, I started by typing documents pertaining to the deaths. After some time there, Micki left, and my sister took her place. She worked there until our contract finished. I still think of that day often and the people who lost their lives that day.

Chapter Eight
WEIRTON STEEL WORKERS

Several men from Weirton Steel were introduced in Chapter 1. Bob Brandt and Jim Black told their stories from their memories of Brown's Island. Jim Black talked of his father Jim Black's experiences on the island. Several of the revelations below come from family members of the workers.

I Tested Water on the Day of the Explosion

Stanley Anthony tells his story to Jane Kraina..

"I worked on the mainland plant on the day of the accident. The sound when the explosion hit reminded me of a cherry bomb firecracker or an M-85. The corrugated building by the filtration plant swayed to one side from the force of the blast.

"I could hear the sirens from the ambulances crossing the bridge. They had their lights on. When they came back, the lights were off, and we knew things were terrible.

"At the time of the explosion, the lab facility where I would work on Brown's Island was preparing for operation but not fully open. I had been testing river water from the river. I worked in the biological treatment of the compounds and ridding them of the bacteria. My job began in 1968 for National Steel in the central lab in the Quality Control Building. My stay on the island lasted for ten years, and then I worked different jobs in environmental control until 2002 when I retired.

"The men's respirators on the new coke plant's job on the island came from the Industrial Hygiene Section of Quality Control. Some people wouldn't wear their masks and equipment to keep them safe.

"Some of the chemical by-products of the coke plant were benzene, naphthalene, xylene, and toluene. The north part of the island contained a pit that stored some of the toxic substances produced from coke making and other steel production waste. I remember that they had to put big concrete slabs across the bridge's length on the Ohio side to stabilize it."

My Uncle Eugene Badis Appeared on the Front Pages of the Newspapers

by nephew Les Halapy as told to Jane Kraina.

"My uncle Eugene 'Gene' Badis received injuries from the Brown's Island explosion. He worked as a Weirton Steel employee for over forty years and belonged to the WSX 25-Year Club. He served as a Merchant Marine during WWII, causing a break in his Weirton Steel employment. He assisted in building the new coke ovens. He inspected brickwork at the time of his accident in his job as a bricklayer. His picture appeared on the cover of the *Weirton Daily Times* and the *Pittsburgh Press*. The photo shows men lifting him from the oven area into the waiting ambulance. The rescue vehicle transported my uncle to the Ohio Valley Hospital in Steubenville, Ohio.

"The *New York Times* also interviewed him on December 15th, 1972. According to what the *New York Times* wrote, Eugene said he was walking along the battery and smelled gas. He began to leave the area, and somebody yelled for him to run. He was only about fifty feet away from the explosion, which he described as sounding like an atomic bomb. The blast blew him twenty feet. He got up and noticed blood running down his face.

"As far as I can remember, my uncle stayed in the hospital for about a week. He suffered cuts, bruises, and burns from the explosion. Although he was not treated for Post Traumatic Stress Disorder, I believed he suffered from the trauma. He had longtime effects. He eventually received a medical retirement.

"Before the incident, he was an outgoing individual who didn't seem like a lot bothered him. After the blast, he withdrew, didn't speak much, and appeared deep in thought. Gene passed away in late December of 1986.

"The rumors I heard regarding the accident blamed the Koppers Company, but my understanding was they never admitted responsibility. People told me that their design had flaws and that the fittings or something like that did not receive proper inspections."

Our Dad Started Working for the Mill when he was Fourteen

Daughters Marge Yenchochic and Marian Grubor
tell their stories to Jane Kraina.

Henry Paravano was general foreman of the Weirton Steel Coke Plant. His daughters tell what they remembered about their father and the explosion.

Marge Yenchochic (daughter of Henry)

"My dad began working for Weirton Steel in 1910. He was only fourteen at the time. Bit by bit, he moved up, finally landing a position as general foreman of the Coke Plant. He retired at age sixty-five after fifty years of service. The mill in their beginning period needed workers, and my father helped to support two families.

"On the day of the accident, people started calling our house. David Kondik called and asked me, 'Where's your dad?'

"I did not know why he was asking. Finally, my father called and said he was okay as well as the rest of our family who worked on the island. Two of my uncles served on the island. My uncle Jim 'Jumbo' Panacci did not go out until the afternoon turn, so he did not witness the explosion but helped in the aftermath. My uncle Pat Cassidy did not get injured, and my cousin's husband Gerald Pearson escaped the dangerous area in time. From what I remember, he was in a car on top of the battery. He was shaken up because the sounds and experience triggered his memories of the Vietnam War. Although our family members all avoided the worst, my father said the situation on the island was catastrophic.

"He helped pull out his friend Bernard Eafrati, who suffered severe injuries. He also was devastated by the loss of his friend Andy Guz." [Note: Both of these men are covered in upcoming chapters.]

"My dad served on an investigating committee that included representatives of all the companies involved. They determined that no one was guilty of malicious negligence. My memories are that Koppers Company was considered most responsible for the accident."

Marian Grubor (daughter of Henry)

"I had just come home from West Liberty, and my mother and I were visiting my sister Marge. While we were there, people kept calling but did not tell us about what had happened. Finally, a neighbor phoned and said to my mother, 'Adeleine, you need to go home. There has been a terrible explosion on the island.' We all returned to my mother's house.

"My father stayed on the island for several days. When my father finally returned home, he talked about the injured men and a man removed from the site who had lost both legs.

"He said, 'For a day or so before the explosion, I knew something wasn't right. I reported it to people who had the power to do something about it, but I felt they didn't take me seriously. I smelled gas. I was up on the battery and ran through the building, warning the men to run.'

"My dad returned home a broken man. As a foreman, he took the brunt of the harsh criticism about the accident. He knew some men were putting the blame where it didn't belong. My dad's nature was stoic, and he was a private person. He always tried to see the good in situations. His workers thought highly of him, but with higher management comes greater responsibility.

"My dad passed away of obstructive coronary disease. The primary chemical that affected his lungs was benzene. He built a vestibule in our house to hang up his work clothes and remove his steel-toed work boots. The smell from his belongings lingered for a long time."

Secrets in the Mist

This bridge spanned the part of the Ohio River that connected West Virginia to Brown's Island. According to workers who walked on the bridge in the winter it could be a cold windy trek. Photo by Dennis Jones.

Chapter Nine

THE MAN WITH THE FLASHLIGHT

written by Joseph Eafrati for his dad Bernard Eafrati.

"Dad was sitting in his favorite chair, a green and white chair with flowers on it. It was a roundish chair that matched the couch my mother was lying on it that night. I was sitting on the floor beside my dad, and we were all watching television. This was the night before the accident. This is the night that I will never forget as long as I live, and here is why.

"My mother was falling asleep. She said she wasn't, but she was doing a great job of drowning out the television with her snoring. Dad and I were trying to get her to go to bed. It was getting late. I had to get up for school the next day, so I touched my dad's hand lightly and said goodnight. He said he was going to go to bed also because he had to get up for work in the morning. He woke mom, and they went to bed. To this day, I cannot touch my dad's hand like that again, fearing that something might happen to him again.

"The next morning was just like any other morning. I went downstairs, and my dad was already up, getting ready for work. It was a dreary December morning, lightly raining and dense cloud cover. Dad was drinking his coffee, and I was making my usual eight waffles for breakfast when mom yelled to dad, 'Don't go to work today because my back hurts and you might have to take me to the doctor's office today.' Dad, who never missed a days' work in thirty years, told her if she gets any worse to call him home at work and he would take her. After dad left for work, I asked mom if she wanted me to stay home with her, and she said no, she would be fine. Thinking back on that conversation, we know now that if he had listened to her, he would not have gotten hurt.

"I finished breakfast and told mom I would be home early from school. It was my senior year, and all I had was two classes. My first class was a carpentry class which was located at the old post office building right behind the fire station. At approximately 9:40 A.M, I was running a board through the jointer trimming the sides when I saw all of the fire trucks rolling out of the station heading north on County Road. I thought they had a terrible house fire somewhere. Then I saw more fire trucks and ambulances and volunteers heading north on County Road.

"Not knowing the tragedy that had just happened to our community, I finished that class and went to my next class up at Weir Sr. High located on Weirton Heights. Ironically, that class was the senior English class that my cousin Beth Digregerio taught. Neither one of us knew that a tragedy had hit our family. When I arrived home at 11:30 A.M, I saw a house full of people. There were neighbors, aunts, and uncles. My older brother Anthony, who took me straight into the kitchen to tell me that there was a severe explosion where our dad works. None of us knew anything more than that.

"Mom was lying on a bed we had set up in our living room because her back was still hurting her. She was crying because of not knowing if he was all right or not. We started getting atrocious calls from people who heard rumors that dad died or had his legs cut off. Those calls really frightened my mother that much more. A neighbor of ours who also worked in that area called and said that there were a lot of people waiting in line to use the phone and dad might be standing in line, too. So, all we could do is wait for word.

"Weirton Steel always had a policy that if an employee were injured or killed on the job, two safety men would go to their home to notify the family. That's one site that our family hoped we would never see. At approximately 2:10 P.M. that afternoon, we saw precisely the sight we never wanted to see. Two men were walking up the front steps to the door. From where I was standing, I could see them coming up the front steps to the door. My heart fell to my knees; I had a deep fear that they were going to say the worse had happened. My mom screamed when she saw them, 'He's dead, he's dead.'

"As the men entered the house, they heard her screaming and said, 'No, no. He's fine. We have the good purpose of telling you he just has a broken leg. He was helping someone out of the blast area, when he fell and broke his leg. He is at the Ohio Valley Hospital.' It felt like a ton of bricks was lifted off our shoulders. A big sigh came over all of us and smiles came back to our faces.

"Anthony told mom to stay home, since she wasn't feeling good. He said his friend Dave Brulla would drive us to the hospital. On the ride over there, I sat in the back seat, holding back tears of joy. When I looked at my brother, I saw him staring out of the window, and tears were dripping down his cheek. These were tears of joy, no doubt. When we arrived at the emergency room, we asked to see our dad. The nurse at the desk told us he was in surgery, and he would be taken to the intensive care unit. They were busy from all the victims of the blast that had less severe injuries. The whole E.R. was buzzing with people; it was traumatic to see so many injured people.

"On the elevator to the ICU, I turned to my brother and said, 'I can't understand why they would put him in intensive care just for a broken leg. Usually, they place the most serious cases there.' When we asked one of the nurses if we could see our dad, she said he was still in the O.R. He had been there since early in the morning, and I felt something was very wrong.

"Late that afternoon we finally got to see him. The afternoon nurse thought that the daylight nurse prepared us for what we were about to see, but she didn't. We peeked in the room and saw four beds. The one closest to us had a person with a leg that was wrapped and hung by cables. I thought that must be him, but I couldn't see his face because they had him lying on his back and his leg was blocking my view. Anthony went in first. I followed him, and Stan followed me. When we rounded the bed, I looked at him and looked at the others. Then I turned to the nurse and asked her, 'Well, where's my dad?'

"She said, 'Right there' pointing to the person in the bed beside me. As I looked at him, he was plugged to monitors, and a respirator was helping him breathe. He had no facial features, his hair was burned off, his head and neck were swollen twice their normal size, and he had a trachea tube in his throat. I couldn't take this for one second longer. I ran out to Linda bawling my head off. I hugged her and told her I didn't even know my own dad.

"Stan came running out, crying just as hard as I was. Later, he told me the nurses had to help him out of there when he saw dad. Anthony was like a rock; he kept his composure and just sat in the chair beside dad's bed and stared at the horrible sight. A few hours had passed while we were in the chapel praying for our dad. When we went out into the hall, Mom had stepped off the elevator with my uncle Dominick, who drove her over to the hospital. Anthony had to explain to mom what my dad looked like. He warned her it wasn't going to be easy seeing him in this condition. We explained everything to her so she wouldn't be shocked as we were. She went in and stayed with him a while, and surprisingly, she remained calm and steady. When she came out, that's when she broke down. We all went into the chapel to pray for him. Lord knows he needed all the prayers we had to give.

"The rest of the relatives and friends were coming in at that time, and we had a long talk with them also. The doctors informed us straight out that they really didn't think he was going to make it. They said he had multiple cuts, broken bones, 1st, 2nd, and 3rd-degree burns, scorched lungs, and ruptured eardrums. Since he was rejecting the blood transfusions, that didn't give us much hope.

"As time passed, my uncles told jokes in the waiting room to break up the sadness. Well, just saying my uncles weren't natural comedians. They made us laugh because they would butcher the joke so much, it made it funnier. They were loving, caring people.

"Later that evening, when I gathered myself back together, I went back to see him. As I stood beside his bed, I grabbed his hand and held it. I looked at his face, shiny from all the burn lotion. As I stared at all the monitors they had him hooked up to, I felt helpless. Staring down at him, I saw him open his eyes and say, 'Joe.' His eyes were a light blue, and I thought, 'Wait a minute, his eyes should be brown.' He could barely get my name out because of his trachea tube in his throat. Right then, I knew he was fighting for his life with every ounce of energy he had left. I just smiled and started talking to him. I know he was happy that I was there with him. He really didn't know how bad off he really was. When I went out to the waiting room, I commented to my brother that dad had blue eyes. He said, 'No, he has brown eyes.' I know he wasn't blind because he recognized me. After a while, his eyes turned back to brown.

"Ten more days and Christmas would be here. It wasn't much of a Christmas, but as I look back at it, it was the best Christmas ever because God gave us our dad back. Over those ten days, it was touch-and-go every day. The doctors would tell us to call a priest for his last rites. Then he would pull out of it. Then they said, 'Call the family; he took a turn for the worse.' Then he would get better. It was like a roller coaster ride up, one day and down the next.

"Christmas morning we went to see him, and they had his head propped up. The staff had pulled his trachea tube out and were feeding him Jell-O. They also had a little Christmas tree on a table where we put his gifts. That's when the doctor decided to take him out of ICU and put him in a private room on the same floor with twenty-four-hour nurses.

"My sister Susan lived in Hawaii, and we had to call her with the news. It was a living hell for her not being in Weirton. She didn't know if she would ever see him alive again. She didn't get here until about a week later. We told dad she was coming in for Christmas. She didn't want him to see her earlier for fear that he would know how bad he was.

"Our cousin Buddy DiGregorio had gotten married, and he and his new bride came over to see dad. They had just left the ceremony, and they were still in their wedding attire. He was overjoyed to see them; it made his day. That is what people thought of him and loved him so much to do something like that.

"At home on Christmas day, we sat down at the dinner table, and Anthony sat at my dad's chair. When we started to eat, he broke down and cried. He just couldn't sit there any longer. The day after Christmas, we were all at the hospital to watch them move him to his room. He was excited because he had a window, and we could stay with him as long as we wanted."

WHY?

"One day he asked again how his buddies were doing. He thought they were as bad as him, and that is why he couldn't see them. We brought the doctor in, and with all of us around him, the doctor told him that they didn't make it out alive. From that day on, he asked why he survived and not them. They call that reaction Survivor's Remorse. It haunted him for the rest of his life. I remember the wife and son of one of his buddies who died coming to see him, and he was happy to see them.

"We heard of all kinds of rumors of what caused the accident but never knew what my dad actually went through until he was able to talk about it. He began to tell us the gruesome story: 'Three of us were on top of the coke battery getting readings when we smelled coke gas. Then the helper came up to tell us he smelled gas also. He then went back to the reversing room, and we proceeded down to the basement to look for gas leaks. I stayed near the stairwell looking for leaks and the other two men went straight and to the right. When I looked up, both of them were staggering back towards me. One of them fell on the floor, and the other fell into my arms. I knew then I had to carry him up the stairs to get fresh air. I started dragging him up the steps when I was overcome with gas and passed out also. When I came to, I realized that I had fallen down the steps over the railing and onto the floor. From my waist up, I was under the stairs with my legs sticking out. I looked up and saw the other man lying on the steps above me. Then there was a tremendous explosion; it was the loudest thing I ever heard. Even the bombs when I served in WWII weren't as loud as that.

"That knocked me out again. As I came to, I realized I was burning. My arms were burning, and my pants were completely burned off from the upper thigh down. There were six inches of water on the floor, and I used that to put out the fire on my arms and chest. The flames kept enveloping me, and when I looked up to see where it was coming from, I saw the horrendous sight of my friend burning to death right above me on the steps.

"I tried moving, but my legs were trapped under a big piece of concrete half the size of my hospital bed. The concrete had a handrail on it. I knew I had to get out of there. I started to lift the cement, but it was too heavy. I prayed for help, and I swear angels were helping me raise it. I lifted it an inch and threw small chunks of cement under it and kept doing that until it was high enough to pull my right leg out, but my left leg was still stuck. I then knew that the railing was protruding through the concrete and through my ankle. Then I did the only thing I could--yank it until I was free. When I finally pulled it out, my foot was hanging on by the skin. I knew the foot was hopeless, and I couldn't walk on it.

"After crawling halfway, I found a board to use for a crutch. I couldn't get up the steps, so I decided to go through the double steel doors that led under the battery of coke ovens. I thought if I could make it to the other side, there was a set of steps I could escape from. I had a hard time standing and walking, so I tried reaching up to hold on to pipes, but there was fire curling on the ceiling. I went through the doors and hobbled as far as I could, but it was no use. I moved ten feet and slid down into the water.

I couldn't go any further, so I sat down on a steel wagon about halfway through the basement. I tried moving it with my good leg, but it was too heavy. I thought my heart was going to explode. I felt, my God, I'm going to need help getting out of here. I lay down on the wagon, pulled out my flashlight from the holder on

The Man with the Flashlight

my belt, and started waving it and yelling for someone to help me. I was hoping someone would see the light through the thick smoke that was filling the basement.

"There were two men from the Steubenville Ambulance Company that were looking through a fence that surrounded the coke battery. They spotted my light and ran around the south stairwell. A security officer stopped them from going in. He said it was going to blow a second time. The two men then ran back around and cut through the fence and sneaked down around the officer and went down into the dark smokey basement. Then they saw my light faintly in the distance. I heard them sloshing toward me through the water. When I looked up and saw them, they were like two angels sent by God himself. They laid the stretcher down in the water and placed me on it. As they were carrying me out, I kept saying, 'My buddies are in there.' After they loaded me into the ambulance, they went back in, and then it blew again. They got knocked down and slightly burned but made it out all right.

"The last thing I remember is the ambulance ride to the hospital. We went up a steep hill, and the stretcher I was on broke loose and headed for the door. The ambulance attendant grabbed it and held it until we reached the hospital.

"My dad went through a lot of pain and suffering. The hardest part for me was going down to the burn tank where they immersed him in water and peeled his dead skin off. He cringed in pain. The nurse told him. 'Honey, it's OK to cry. They all do.' He did, and I did. It was difficult to stand helpless and watch him in pain and agony.

"The hospital staff put a walking cast on his foot. We watched him learn how to walk again, one step at a time. He lost a lot of weight and muscle and didn't look like himself. When they finally released him after five months in the hospital, they carried him home on a stretcher. The neighbors were there to cheer him on and give him a big welcome home. I remember my young niece was afraid of the cast on his leg and my dad being in a wheelchair.

"I was really excited when I saw him at my graduation ceremony that June in a wheelchair. I had to be the happiest kid there.

"While he was in the ICU, a candy striper came up to asked me if that was my dad and I said yes. She said how sorry she was to see our family suffering. Then she said it was over fast for her. She said that her dad was with my dad in the basement and didn't survive. All I could do was stare at her. Here she was consoling me when her dad had died that day. It put me in shock."

CONCLUSION

"I wrote this story for my dad; this December will be twenty years since the accident. Since then, he has been pretty good. He still walks with a cane, and he never could go back to work. He likes his garden, and he makes wood crafts to keep busy. I've never felt closer to my dad as I do now. He is always there for me, and I take his advice on any project I have going on. Thanks, Dad, for being there when I need you. Our prayers go out for the nineteen men who lost their lives.

"My dad is gone now. He passed away in 2007 at the age of 88. The accident happened to him when he was 54. One odd thing I noticed: he worked 34 years in the mill, and he lived 34 years after the accident. I thank God every day that my children got to grow up knowing him. My sister Linda started having kids soon after the accident, so he would get to see them.

Some additional information from Anthony Eafrati, Joe's brother

I remember when I entered the hospital room to see my father. As Joe, said he was unrecognizable. The fire from the explosion burned eighty-five percent of his body and seared his lungs. His eyebrows were burned off. His head looked like a glazed donut. When he pulled himself as far as could he used his arms to "walk."

Our house then was on Fifth Street in Weirton. You could throw a rock and hit the old coke plant. When my father was younger Brown's Island had been his "playground." People swam over to the island from the north end location of Weirton.

Bernard Eafratti's pension struggles are detailed in Chapter 11: "The Aftermath"

Chapter Ten

THOSE WHO DIED

The officials' first concern was to check the workers' roll calls on the island to determine the missing and injured. Retrieving the bodies and protecting the site from experiencing additional explosions was paramount. The security men on the site denied access to the press and visitors at this time. Family members waited on the Ohio side of the bridge. Ambulances and their medical staff on the island sent men with serious health concerns to the hospitals. Firefighters and other rescue workers helped with lifting men out of the rubble and placing them in ambulances.

Workers on the island stayed or returned later to help with finding remains. Some men spooked by the event, drove off the island and never came back. One man headed for Cleveland and stayed there.

The following lists those who died as a result of the explosion:

Weirton Steel of West Virginia employees

- Andy Guz, 48, Weirton, West Virginia, heater at the Old Coke Plant, World War II navy veteran. Survived by his wife Patricia (Talbot), a daughter Linda, and a son Andy

- Samuel Morgart, Jr., 45, Steubenville, Ohio, a heater in

the Coke Plant, a deacon in North River Avenue Church of Christ. Survived by his wife, Shirley (Monat), a son Thomas, and a daughter Chirl Ann

Yobe Electric Company of Sharon, Pennsylvania

- Members of IBEW 246

- Edward (Dick) Arthurs, 56, Toronto, Ohio, electrician, member of First United Methodist Church, American Legion Post, and IBEW. Survived by his wife Beryle (Tuttle) and a son Richard Burns

- Howard Bray, 44, Toronto, Ohio, electrician, member of Ambassador Quartet, WWII and Korean War veteran. Survived by his wife Doris (Wells) and two daughters, Sheryle and Susan (Schultz)

- James Brown, 31, Toronto, Ohio, electrician, member of United Presbyterian Church, was on the Toronto Titans' coaching staff. Survived by his wife, Sharon (Bushanic), a son James and a daughter Christine

- Robert K. (Kenny) Gaines, 29, Wellsburg, West Virginia, electrician, served in U.S. Army, 1962-1964, member Wellsburg Moose, a representative of Trades and Labor Union, IBEW Local 246. Survived by his wife Sharon (Boehl,) a son Ramon, and daughter Tara Kay

- Arthur McCort {XE "McCort, Arthur"}, electrician, St. Clairsville, Ohio, was a member of St. Mary's Catholic Church, St. Clairsville, and the Toledo, Ohio, Local Union of Electricians. Survived by his wife, Beverly (Clark), a daughter, Melissa, and a son, Arthur, Jr.

- Lou Sommers, 33, Wintersville, Ohio, electrician, member of

Brentwood United Methodist Church, manager of the Little League team in Wintersville, IBEW Local 246. Survived by Karen (McClave), and three sons, Jeffrey, Brian, and Robbie

George Hamilton Company of Pennsylvania

- Members of Asbestos Union Local #2

- Paul Byrne, 32, Pittsburgh, Pennsylvania, asbestos worker

- Michael Crowley, 26, asbestos worker

- Russell Ober, 55, Pittsburgh, Pennsylvania, asbestos worker, WWII veteran

- Michael Repko, 45, asbestos worker, Coraopolis, Pennsylvania

- Albert Tuttle, 34, Pittsburgh, Pennsylvania, asbestos worker. Survived by wife Marjorie (Ferris) and a son Brian

- James Tuttle, 44, Pittsburgh, Pennsylvania, asbestos worker. Survived by wife Wilma (Smith), a son, James, and a daughter, Kathryn

- Note: Albert and James Tuttle were brothers

Koppers Co. of Pennsylvania

- John Toms, 26, McKeesport, Pennsylvania, engineering operator. Survived by his parents, John and Mary Toms

- David Van Sickle, 23, safety administrator and supervisor, Wintersville, Ohio. He grew up in Kansas.

- William Kliner, 59, pipefitter, Steubenville, Ohio. Survived by his wife Ella Marie (Harmon), five sons, William, James, Harry, Edward, Robert, and a daughter, Marian

- Note: William Kliner was a member of Pipefitter/Welder, Local Union 490

- Kenneth Harris, 51, laborer foreman from Rayland, Ohio

- Note: Kenneth Harris was a member of the Laborers Union 809

Bowers Tile and Marble Company

- Charles E. Bowers, 27, Richmond, Ohio, tile fitter, survived by his parents Charles and Peggy (Homan) Bowers

- The accident injured workers, and some of them required treatment at area hospitals. The following men were sent to Ohio Valley Hospital: Bernard Eafrati, Leo Frazier, Joseph Veraldi, Eugene Badis, Raymond Davis, Charles Bensi, and James Ghenne.

- Deno Galanios went to St. John Medical Center. Weirton General Hospital released and treated Kenneth Poorman and Wilson Bordner.

A Place of Fun and then Fatality

Barry Brown tells Jane Kraina about his brother Jim who perished.

"Three members of my family worked on the island on December 15, 1972. My dad, my brother, Jim and I belonged to the IBEW 246 Union of electricians. We worked for the Yobe Company from Sharon, Pennsylvania, who employed us to work on the island. The thick and foggy air lay still, and the lack of movement added to the problem of gas unable to disperse.

"My brother and I had begun our breaks. I took mine up on

top of the batteries and Jim took his in the electrical control room. Our bosses up on the batteries told us to get down and head to the south of the area. I was about thirty yards away from the ovens when the gas explosion hit.

"I began to look for my brother Jim. I was encouraged when somebody told me they had seen him recently. It proved to be a short-lived feeling as he had perished in the break area.

"On this particular day, operations were in a transition period, readying the Weirton Steel employees to take over running the ovens and coking procedures. Because some of the men were watching others work, they gave the impression to one worker on the top that they were standing around doing nothing. A younger worker on the top, whose job involved checking for gas leaks, said, 'If they aren't doing anything down there, I am not going to do anything either'. I don't remember who the worker was, but I have some anger over his negligent attitude.

"I was also bothered by the attitude that production took precedence over safety. With the new OSHA guidelines coming out, the companies were taking safety a little more seriously as penalties came in the form of fines. But I know supervisors still had to always worry about production, and sometimes there was a pause about stopping workers. In the case of the explosion, it seemed to me that there was a delay in taking action. They surmised that escaping gas affected the workers as men started passing out in the scaffolding area, but I felt they could have told them to leave a little earlier than they did.

"Even today, I see a slowness to correct safety issues in some companies. Workers can complain about issues, but it takes a severe injury or death to spur action. Then, of course, correction comes quickly.

"Sharon, Jim's wife, and a son and daughter survived him. He was only thirty-one when he died. Jim belonged to the United Presbyterian Church in Toronto, and he also served on the coaching staff of the Toronto Titans. Koppers Company did compensate his widow, but it wasn't a large settlement. Interestingly, my brother usually bought Christmas presents for his family at the last minute. In December of 1972, he had purchased and wrapped all the gifts before December 15.

"My father had experienced a nervous breakdown before the accident and working on the island was his start to getting back to work. The accident devastated him, and he suffered another bout of frayed nerves.

"I did not return to the island to work immediately after the accident. My brother Jim and I had camped on the island before our job there. I continued to camp there afterward. Weirton Steel only charged about five dollars to rent a lot. Both sides of the island contained these lots.

"I also returned about twenty years after the explosion to do a small electrical job on the island. Only two of us worked on that project. It gave me a creepy feeling."

A Twist of Fate

Pat Byrne, nephew of Paul Byrne, who died in the explosion, tells his story to Jane Kraina.

"I am the nephew of Paul Byrne, who died in the explosion. I recall clearly the events surrounding my uncle's death. Ironically, my uncle tried ardently to get me on the island to work. My uncle was 32 and was a sweetheart of a man. We had both trained as Asbestos Insulators and belonged to Asbestos Workers Local #2 in Pittsburgh, Pennsylvania. He failed in getting me employed on the island, so I went to work for Congo Company up in Newell, West Virginia. I got laid off from there and ended up going to Mt. Storm in West Virginia.

Paul, one of six brothers, had just told me to be careful in Mt. Storm. He said to me, 'Keep your nose clean. Stay out of the bars and watch the women. Give me a call when you get home.'

"When my friend and I drove home for the weekend, we heard an announcement on the car radio about an explosion in Weirton, West Virginia. Not thinking of the possibility of it being on the island, I said to this friend, 'It's a shame that West Virginia has so many tragedies at Christmas. Point Pleasant's 'Silver Bridge' collapsed five years earlier, right before Christmas.'

"I was staying at my grandmother's house in Pittsburgh. When I arrived there, all the lights were on. I called his sister and asked, 'Where's Nanny?'

She responded, 'You haven't heard? Your uncle was killed!'

"Interestingly, my other uncle Patrick Byrne also worked on the island that day. It was raining and miserable, and the boss had said the men could go home if they wanted or stay on the island. Paul chose to keep working, and Patrick went home. After Patrick heard about the explosion, he got back in his car and returned to the island.

"My uncle Paul was the oldest son in his family. I was the youngest of the offspring of the brothers. Paul chose me to be the godfather of his son. Back then, the godparents had to talk to the priest before the baptism.

"Paul's other son was just eighteen months old when my godson was born, and I thought being a godfather would be an 'easy gig,' especially since his uncle had moved to a new house with a pool. My uncle had moved away from the North Side, where all his other brothers lived, and they made fun of him for doing so.

"The priest said that being a godfather was a serious responsibility. He added that you never knew what life would bring. I always remembered these words as I lived my life.

"Paul's wife never remarried, but she did an excellent job of raising their two sons. One became a vice president at PNC Bank, and the other is a professor at a university and heads up the Mechanical Engineering Division."

The Nineteenth Victim

Mary Lynn Mitchell, sister of Robert Gaines, tells her story to Mary Zwierchowski.

Robert Kennon Gaines of Wellsburg was killed in the Coke Plant explosion on Brown's Island, December 15, 1972. Of the 19 men who lost their lives that day, his body was the last to be recovered.

Left behind were his wife Sharon (Boel) Gaines and two young children, Raymond and Tara Kay. Surviving also were his parents, Robert and Virginia (Booher) Gaines and a sister Mary Lynn (Gaines) Mitchell.

Mary Lynn shared her memories of that tragic day. "We called him 'Kenny.' He was 29 years old when the accident happened. He was employed as an electrician with Yobe Electric and was a member of IBEW Local 246. Kenny liked his job and enjoyed spending time with his buddies. He was outgoing and fun to be around.

"He rode to work that morning with two other fellows. They said later Kenny seemed unusually quiet. Coffee break was around 9:00 A.M., but he never joined them. Said he wanted to stay and finish what he was doing. He was in the basement of the building when the plant exploded. His friend Richard Ferguson went looking for him but couldn't find him." Kenny would remain missing for eight long agonizing hours.

Mary Lynn retraced her steps on that dreary Friday morning. "It was close to Christmas, so my husband Earl and I went out to do some shopping around town in Wellsburg. I sensed that something was going on. I could hear people talking, but I didn't know what happened. Around 1:00 we headed for Steubenville and were crossing the Market Street Bridge when we heard the news on the radio—something about an explosion and injuries—but it still wasn't clear to me until we got to the Downtown Bakery. Everyone was talking about the explosion on Brown's Island. Then I realized that's where Kenny works."

"All we could do was to go home and wait. I had never heard of Brown's Island until my brother started working there. My father explained that it was somewhere at the north end of Weirton, in the middle of the Ohio River.

By 3:00 P.M., the Gaines family had gathered at Mary Lynn's home. "All we knew at this point was that Kenny was missing," she said. "I could hear Sharon crying in the next room." Word finally came three hours later, around 6:00 P.M. that his body had been recovered and was being held at the Weirton General Hospital. A family member, they said, would have to identify him. "My cousin, Dr. Bill Booher, offered to go alone. Despite Bill's objection, Dad insisted on going with him. 'I need to go,' he said. 'He's my son.' When they returned, my father was quiet. The somber look on his face confirmed the worst. Kenny's body had been found underneath three other bodies. He was the last to be pulled out. They had been crushed by the sudden collapse of steel and concrete.

Visitation was held the next day at Chambers Funeral Home. The casket was closed. Unlike many other casualties of the blast, Kenny's body remained intact. But still, he could not be shown. Mary Lynn recalls, "I remember watching my mother standing there, staring down at the casket and saying 'How do I know that it's really him?' She turned to Bill and asked if he remembered the scar on Kenny's arm (from a boyhood injury) — was it there? Bill gave a slight nod and walked away. Mother knew Kenny was gone. It was just her way of handling her grief.

Services were held at the funeral home Monday morning. Those who attended gathered again in the wintry cold air of Franklin Cemetery as the body of Robert Kennon Gaines was laid to rest.

He was buried just seven days before Christmas. For Mary Lynn and her family, the holiday became a painful time. 'Christmas was terrible,' she said. 'I just wanted it to be over. I remember screaming, 'This can't be Christmas!' My mother calmed me down. It was hard — it was a difficult time for all of us."

When asked if she blamed anyone for the accident, she said, "Yes. I blame Weirton Steel. The smell of gas was heavy that day. They should have shut down the job and located the source of the leak."

Mary Lynn did not know how much compensation, if any, was awarded families of the victims, but she felt that no amount of money could fully compensate for the loss of those 19 innocent lives — and the tremendous pain and sorrow that went along with it.

The Longest Ride of My Life

Andrew Guz, son of Andy Guz Sr., tells his story to Jane Kraina.

"I was visiting my friends at Marshall University in Huntington. Most of the students had cleared out for the Christmas holiday, but my friends and I decided to stay and watch the Christmas Basketball Tournament.

"At noon, on December 15, 1972, my friend Steve Hines told me that he heard that there was an explosion in Weirton Steel and the coke plant was involved. At this point, my heart sank.

"All afternoon, I waited for a phone call. I hoped that everything was OK. We were all getting ready to go to the tournament, and we headed for the store. When I got back to the fraternity house, I got a message from Francis Palumbo, 'Your family wants you to call home.'

"They said, 'Your dad is missing, and you need to come home.' Charlie Garrison and Bill Najedki accompanied me on my drive to Weirton. It was the longest ride of my life.

"When I got home around eight or nine, everyone was there, and they gave me the news that my father died. If it were not for a scheduled coffee break, a lot more men would have perished. My uncle John was also working on the island as a foreman, but he was in the canteen during the explosion. My dad had smelled the gas leak, left the area, and decided to go back into the building to warn people.

"My family felt that the accident was never fully explained. The companies rushed to get the ovens ready before the end of the year. Koppers said that possibly one of the welders had created a spark. However, they never pinned down the cause for us.

"We got a settlement from the Koppers company, which took most of the blame for the explosion. We could not sue the company because there was a law on the books in West Virginia that said you could not sue your employers for an accident unless the harm proved deliberate. Koppers was quick to settle and have things over.

"In 1981, I returned to the island for a party. I did not venture to the site where my father lost his life."

Unsung Hero

William Kliner, son of Ed Kliner, tells his story to
Jane Kraina.

"My dad William was fifty-nine at the time of the accident that took his life. Koppers sub-contracted him as a member of the Local Plumbers and Pipefitters from Steubenville, Ohio. I had graduated from Wayne State in Detroit. I started working in Chillicothe, Ohio, so I was away from the Steubenville area when the Brown's Island accident occurred. I was twenty-seven. My brother James also worked as a pipefitter. He went out on the afternoon shift the day of the explosion.

"I married in 1968. My wife Carole and I traveled around the country in the summer months, which made us happy and ready to have children by 1972. My father had come to visit and helped us put the baby bed together a few weeks before the accident. My first child was born on November 11, but my father never got a chance to see his grandson, Joshua.

"I had just started working for Goodwill Rehabilitation Program, and I was in the middle of a meeting when my mother tried to reach me. After the session, I could see the long faces of my coworkers, and the secretary notified me to contact my mother.

"My father, a foreman, did not work directly at the coke oven battery that morning but was on another part of the island, but he made his way to the site where he saw people lying on the ground overcome by the gas leakage. He rushed into the basement area to help pull people out of the pit. He helped one person out and then returned to get another man. This time he did not come out as the explosion blasted the area he had entered, and he was fatally injured.

"When I got home from my job, my wife had our bags packed, and we drove to my mother's house. My mother did receive a settlement from Koppers Company."

Our Family Looked Up to Him

Fred Ober, cousin of Russell "Gabby" Ober, tells his story to Jane Kraina.

"My cousin Russell Ober was the oldest person from Hamilton Co. on the job at 60 years of age. Although he was my cousin, I thought of him as my uncle. He lived with my family at times. We considered him the hero of our family. Drafted by the military, he fought in the Infantry Forces for four years and received an Army Bronze Star.

"Outnumbered and surrounded for five days, a U.S. Army combined arms force of airborne infantry, armor, engineers, tank destroyers, and artillery conducted a successful defense of the Belgian crossroads town of Bastogne in late December 1944. They separated the German combined arms formations and destroyed the sections, halting the offensive. The outcome of this Battle of the Bulge was critical to the victorious Allied defenses against the German Ardennes offenses. (from Book on Bastogne)

"After surviving the harsh conditions of World War II, he died on Brown's Island in the United States. He would never enjoy retirement. He had three children who were due to graduate in 1972. One of his sons graduated from law school, his daughter from West Virginia, and his other son from Bucknell. I got the call while I was at work. The Asbestos Union #2 in Pittsburgh had planned a financial meeting for that night. I went to the local office that afternoon, and they told me the details.

"Like other asbestos workers, he took his break in the basement area where the explosion caused the concrete to trap the men in the lethal gas. The heavy moisture produced by the rain did not allow the gas leaking into the area to disperse. My first reaction was that I needed to go over to see Russell's wife and tell her the news. I rounded up the kids. I went to Weirton General Hospital to help identify the body. I was looking for his clothing as he had a stocky build. The rescue workers found his body first as it lay closest to the door. The injury decapitated him.

"The funeral home closed his casket, but his two sons wanted to see him. Our family endured great sadness for a time. I attended everybody's funeral from the union. The men were a close-knit group.

"One of his friends, Fred Coll, who witnessed the blast, vowed he would never quit smoking because the cigarettes saved his life. He had gone out to smoke. He finally stopped later in his life."

A Flip of the Coin

Sandy Reducah, brother of Lou Sommers, tells her story to Jane Kraina.

"My brothers Lou and Jim Sommers worked as electricians, and both belonged to the local IBEW 246 out of Steubenville. My mother had nine children--five boys and four girls. Lou was the oldest at 33 in 1972, and his brother Jim was 31. They slept in the same bed until Lou got married as the family was large. Their relationship was close, being so near in age. Jim looked up to his brother.

"The day of the explosion, they both worked. As the time neared for a coffee break, they flipped a coin to see who would go on the break. Lou lost the coin toss and remained to finish up some work. As Jim neared the site after the break, the explosion hit. Jim was only a hundred yards away. For Jim the trauma lasted a lifetime.

"Jim believed he had run away and not helped his brother. For thirty-five years, this thought stayed in his head, tormenting him. Then as he told someone about that fateful day from 1972, the person said, 'What are you talking about, Jim? You stayed and helped dig with sledgehammers and spud bars.'

"My brother Jim eventually went into treatment in Dennison, Ohio, and Dr. Haugh said to us. 'My God, what this man's been through from his guilt about the accident. He has a serious case of PTSD (Post Traumatic Stress Disorder).' Before that, we thought he was bipolar. He did drink to deal with the nightmare his life had become. He had a terrific sense of guilt, which he never got over.

"On the day of the accident, I was Christmas shopping. When I got home, my husband said, ' We have to go to your mom's. They can't find Lou.'

"When they told my mother about Lou, she collapsed on the floor. The two of them had a tight bond. The news devastated her, but in time she recovered from his death.

"My dad and my brother went to the island, and a security cop stopped them. 'You can't go on the island.'

"My dad said, 'You have to let me on. My boy's missing.' The cop let them on.

"The television reporters wanted to speak to my dad. He informed them he did not want to be on TV. They ran the coverage anyway.

"Our family never talked about the accident. My mother quit going to the grocery store because so many people approached her. Wintersville, Ohio is a close-knit community, and everyone knew our family.

"Ed Kliner, whose father Bill was killed in the accident, came to Lou's funeral. The funeral crowd proved so large that they had to put three tiers of scaffolding up at the Dunlop Funeral Home. The funeral home quit accepting flowers as there was no room to hold them.

"Lou left three boys. Karen, his wife, did get a settlement, but it wasn't enough, so she returned to work. At that time, people did not discuss unpleasant events as they do now. Lou's son came to me one day and said, 'I'd like to know more about my dad.'

"I said, 'Go talk to your uncle Jim. He is the one that knows the most about your father. They talked for hours."

Explosion debris in front of door of the room where electricians were trapped. Photo by Harry Porter.

"Just recently, my daughter went to a psychic. The psychic told her, 'You need to go over to the island and sprinkle salt where your uncle died. His spirit does not want to leave the island and his family. He needs to be released.'"

Cement being pushed up from below. Photo by Harry Porter.

Damage would need repaired. Photo by Harry Porter.

Chapter Eleven
AFTERMATH

News Reporting and Investigations

In the December 18,1972 issue of *The Evening Review* (East Liverpool, Ohio), newsmen reported that governor Arch Moore from West Virginia commissioned six men to examine the island for clues on what caused the accident. Two state fire marshals, two state policemen, and two members of the Labor Department arrived to gather information and write a report for the governor. They arrived on the island on Saturday. "It seems to be it would be some number of weeks before they disassemble all the debris, make the necessary repairs and reconstruct the site," said J. D. Higby of the state police. The finding of that final report could not be researched due to COVID closing libraries in the state, particularly the one that holds papers and documents of Arch Moore. Other research was provided, but there was not a report of their investigation.

Security remained tight on the island with newsmen being allowed on the island on Saturday. Koppers held a conference for those on the site that day. On Sunday cleanup began.

Newspapers around the United States covered the explosion on Brown's Island. Walter Cronkite mentioned it on the CBS Evening News. The *New York Times* covered the story for several days. The Pittsburgh papers ran the story for several days, as workers from the Pittsburgh area perished in the accident. Local papers in Steubenville and the Weirton area ran articles for some time.

One of the important questions centered around the cause of the accident. In interviews from those on the island that day and family survivors', the following explanations were revealed. One family had been told that welders had created a spark. Several people pointed to the water seals having defects or failing. This created a pocket of gas, and one person said an unknown spark flared up.

Another worker said the gas holder had problems. Pressure built up and a surge blew the water valve off. Someone else heard the gas preheater feeding fuel to the battery developed a leak and the trapped gas ignited. A similar theory was that pressure inside the gas lines swelled over the acceptable limit; a tar plug on a coke gas line caused a water seal to blow. Another version was that workers hadn't finished connecting one of the gas lines, and the gas escaped out of the open pipe. In addition to that, someone supposedly walked out with a lit cigarette.

An interesting premise was that somebody on the mainland shut off the gas being piped to the island. A family member said an inexperienced worker handled the gas flow. Also, some questioned the valve itself.

On December 21, 1972, the *Pittsburgh Post-Gazette* revealed that The Occupation Safety and Health Administration (OSHA) would investigate the coke oven explosion occurring during Koppers construction. Chain Robbins, deputy assistant secretary of labor and OSHA administrator, said a team would "attempt to find the cause of the accident and what safety standards were involved and ways to insure an accident does not happen again."

In 2013, a discussion of "Historic Workplace & Environmental Health and Safety Films" noted some of the actions OSHA investigated and claimed the protective group "issued eleven citations against five firms with penalties totaling $6,200." The citations included failure to provide adequate means of limiting exposure to flammable, combustible, explosive, and asphyxiating coke oven gas. Also, they noted a neglect to provide a safe exit should a fire occur. The companies failed to prohibit employees from smoking in the vicinity of the coke oven gas distribution piping system." These listing of faults provide some of the activities contributing to the explosion.

Another investigation involved a seven-man team of Koppers, Weirton Steel employees, and consulting firms. The Weirton Steel man listed the participants as follows: "Basil Hinchcliffe, chief project engineer of Koppers Engineering and Construction Division; Andrew Fraser project engineer with Weirton Steel; Henry Paravano, by-product general foreman with Weirton Steel; Philip Metz, assistant vice president of Johnson and Higgins insurance brokerage firm; Ronald T. Jones, engineer with Douglas G. Peterson and Associates, an engineering consulting firm; Frances Schachte, operations analyst with Koppers; and John Porada, safety director of Koppers Engineering and Construction Division. Henry Paravano's daughter remembered that the outcome showed no malicious intent, but Koppers bore a little more of fault in the explosion.

On December 22, 1972, the *Weirton Daily Times* reported on the investigation proceedings regarding the coke oven explosion occurring just a week before. Koppers Company revealed, "coke oven gas was the explosive medium for the accident." The gas had leaked in the basement area of the northernmost end of the ovens and nineteen feet beyond that.

At the time of their interview, they had not found the precise location of the leak.

The Occupational Safety and Health Administration (OSHA) was also looking into the accident. A seven-man team put together a group who gave some theories on the igniting factor for the gas to explode: metal-to-metal spark, an electrical spark, a lighted cigaret, welding equipment, or several others.

The fact-finding group inspected pipes, equipment, and other apparatus. They interviewed workers who had been in the vicinity of the explosion. They had smelled the gas odor before the deadly blast.

Heroes

In the *Weirton Steel Bulletin*, J. H. Harris, Chairman and President of Weirton Steel, lauded the efforts of rescue teams for their valiant actions. He said, "The company is sincerely grateful for the valorous efforts of all those who participated in rescue work during the tragedy. Especially, the ambulance crews and volunteer firemen who demonstrated extraordinary courage and gallantry in putting themselves in peril to rescue victims. Plainly, their efforts were above and beyond the call of duty.

"Also, the company is deeply appreciative of the cooperation and concerned action of the personnel of area hospitals, area police and firemen, West Virginia State Police, the Independent Guard Union, West Virginia Governor Arch A. Moore, Jr. and the news media."

In an earlier chapter of this book, Bernard Eafrati's son told the tale of his father's remarkable rescue and recovery. Two men who helped him, John C. Bowers and Harvey Templin of Steubenville, Ohio, received the Carnegie Hero Award by meeting the requirement of "A civilian who voluntarily risks his or her own life, knowingly, to an extraordinary degree while saving or attempting to save the life of another person is eligible for recognition by the Carnegie Hero Fund Commission." Jeanne Noe, a nurse at the scene, was also nominated for the award but did not receive it. John Bowers and Harvey Templin had earlier received commendation from Dr. John Cashman, director of the Ohio Department of Health, for their rescuing four men from the burning building, disregarding orders and risking their lives. James Deganhart of the Brilliant Volunteer Fire Department was also given an award.

Bowers and Templin's award stated that they "helped to rescue Bernard Eafrati and assisted in rescue of others following an explosion, West Virginia, December 15, 1972. When an explosion occurred at a coke plant, Eafrati, 54, and other workmen were severely injured and unable to get out of the basement as fire spread amid the debris."

Each man "ignored warnings about a possible second explosion and, with another ambulance attendant, entered the basement. With flashlights for the only illumination, they located Eafrati near the basement section where the explosion had occurred. After carrying Eafrati to the basement stairs, from where others took him outside, each man went back to get other injured workmen, but another explosion prevented them from doing so. Eafrati recovered."

Lawsuits

Settlements were given to families. Many did not have the money or time to file legal action, as they had young children or other family members in immediate need of support. Some lawsuits ensued as the result of the accident, and two of the suits are included here.

In the *Weirton Daily Times* on November 10, 1973, a reporter wrote that Leo Frazier and his wife Bonnie filed a suit of more than four million dollars against National Steel, Yobe Electric Company, and George V. Hamilton Company. National Steel also sought judgment against Koppers. Callie Tsapis allowed the defendants to view the blast site.

In the September 19, 1975 issue of the *Pittsburgh Post Gazette*, reporters told of a settlement suit on behalf of six of the nineteen workers who died in the coke oven explosion. The families claimed the explosion would not have taken lives if the company had installed a gas meter that detected the odor. It would have cost between $4,000 to $37,000. They did not include the exact amount of money given to families due to pending legislation.

In 1982 a decision made by the judge regarding an appeal from Mr. Peneschi who had jumped from a water tower to the ground and sustained injuries offers the following account of the accident. "Fuel gas was first introduced into the Brown's Island coke battery in August 1972, and the process of heating up the batteries continued until December 1972, the date of the explosion. The fuel gas used to heat the batteries was produced by National at its mainland coke plant that was located in Hancock County, West Virginia, near the river bank across Brown's Island. The gas produced at that plant was pumped under pressure, through gas mains across a bridge and onto Brown's Island. There was a temporary reducing station at the point the fuel gas lines entered the basement of the Brown's Island coke oven battery and made their way through that structure to the flues or burners.

On December 15, 1972, gas escaped from the preheater

washing system (that had no warning or protective devices of any kind) and its attendant drain because the drains of the base of the heater were not closed. The pit into which the drain lines emptied did not have a continuously maintained level of liquid as a seal or lid, nor a vent pipe to carry any escaping gas. The explosion resulted."

Mr. Joseph Peneschi, a Koppers employee, had previously sued National Steel, along with Yobe Electric and George Hamilton Electric, subcontractors of Koppers. and in this appeal, he added Koppers. The first suit was in 1978. That case found in favor of Yobe and Hamilton, electrical subcontractors. They also found National Steel absolved of negligence.

The decision was based on a history of workers taking on the risk of dangerous jobs by signing contracts and taking the job. The employees are rewarded with salary and other benefits. "Thus, a plaintiff who accepts employment driving a tank truck full of nitroglycerin, with knowledge of the danger must be taken to assume the risk when he is injured by an explosion."

The judge found against the plaintiff. The two independent contractors of Koppers, George V. Hamilton, Inc., and Yobe Electric Company were dismissed by the trial court who found they were not negligent. They also considered that they had employees on the job "who might have been smoking and who might have ignited the gas that exploded." Interestingly, "the plaintiffs' own expert testified that there was no defect in the design at the coke battery and the evidence is conclusive that the employees on the construction site knew that gas was escaping and that a dangerous situation was developing.

Another result from the explosion involved changes to people who had disability and then went on social security at age 65. In

Bernard Eafrati's case, he then lost his pension. The family tried to get this corrected, but they failed in getting the pension for Bernard. The Independent Steelworkers Union did see the travesty of this situation, and they were able to add a clause to the Union contract that men would receive their pensions in this situation. They named the addition the "Eafrati clause."

The real loss after the explosion was to families who lost their relatives, and to survivors who suffered mental aftereffects of the explosions. For some, their lives never returned to normal. In a little more than a decade after the blast, the steel industry faltered, and the whole Ohio Valley would be painfully affected by the loss of thousands of industrial jobs.

William Kiefer Gives His Point of View on Accident

After finishing this chapter and as we were finishing up the book, William Kiefer gave us this piece. He was a past attorney for Bogarad and Robertson and Weirton Steel Company; of counsel for two practices in Weirton. He serves as General Counsel for Bethany College, West Virginia.

The Coke Plant explosion on Brown's Island resulted in tremendous loss of life and on top of the fatalities, another forty to sixty people suffered serious injuries. At the time of the blast, the coke oven battery itself was relatively complete and was in heat-up phase. Koppers' operators were in charge of the heat-up and National/Weirton hourly and supervisory personnel where on-site learning the operations of the battery. Also, there were many workers still on the Island engaged in the completion of the adjacent by-products plant, and other ancillary items.

In August, 1972 the battery of coke ovens was sufficiently complete that the task of heating the ovens began. This is a slow process, because the silica brick in the ovens has to be heated from ambient temperature, say eighty degrees Fahrenheit on an August day, to an operating temperature of 1650 to 1800 degrees Fahrenheit on the first day of coke production. In order not to crack the brick and ruin the ovens the heat-up process is slow. It begins with putting heating boxes in each oven and eventually progresses to turning on the gas and heating the individual ovens on an empty basis. By December 15, 1972 this heat up process was nearly complete.

The contract between National Steel and Koppers, Inc., was what is known in construction language as a "turnkey" contract. In essence that meant that the builder, in this case Koppers, Inc., was responsible for the project until such time as the owner, National/Weirton Steel, could take over the completed project. The analogy is an owner turning the key to unlock the door of a project and just taking over as everything is running, ship-shape and broom clean, perfect. That turnover had not occurred on December 15, 1972.

In 1972, Koppers, Inc., a Fortune 500 company was not the only designer-builder of these plants in the US. Their main competitor was an entity called Wilputte Company. It was a subsidiary of Allied Chemical Corp, (today named Honeywell) another Fortune 500 company. In my view one advantage that Koppers had in obtaining the bid was that its street address was much closer to National Steel than was the address of Allied Chemical. The latter was addressed in New York City and Morristown New Jersey. Koppers Inc. owned a thirty-four story headquarters building at 7th Avenue and Grant Street in Pittsburgh. It was virtually across the street from US Steel and four blocks from the National Steel Headquarters. I suspect that to the extent that they did not eat in private corporate dining rooms, the executives of Koppers dined frequently at the Duquesne Club in downtown Pittsburgh as did executives of National Steel, US Steel and the rest of the Pittsburgh industrial leaders. Believe me, it is much easier to do a business deal with someone that you see frequently, than it is to do the same deal with a stranger. That is not unethical, illegal or anything else, just as fact of life. It is why there are sales people.

Koppers was eminently qualified to design and build coke plants. However, unlike Allied Chemical/Wilputte they did not generally operate their own coke ovens. I believe both companies were familiar with pre-heaters. What was unusual in this case was the National/Weirton Steel operating practice of using a pressure washing device of their making to clean the Preheater. The washing operation was simplicity itself: (1) Take the preheater off line; (2) Run high pressure water through it to wash it; (3) Open the drain lines to let the water and any condensate run out; (4) Close drain lines; (5) Put preheater back on line. On the morning of December 15, 1972 all this was done, except for step Four. Someone failed to close the drain lines. As a result when the preheater went on line some of the heating gas went out of the four inch drain lines filling the basement with deadly, explosive coke oven gas. The explosion was a natural result.

After the explosion. Because of the deaths and injuries, there were going to be investigations and lawsuits. Anticipating this fact of life, Koppers, in charge of the siteconducted an investigation, or more likely its insurance carrier did so. Why? Because there was millions of dollars in property damage plus all the deaths and injuries. Koppers was the most likely responsible party, and it had insurance. On top of that the turn key contract provided that Koppers had to indemnify National/Weirton for any damages due to third parties which were caused by accidents on the site.

At that time, as today, it was a Plaintiff's burden in a legal claim to establish evidence that they were hurt, and that some party caused that hurt, as a result of a negligent or unlawful act.

Aftermath

There are Rules of Civil Procedure in force in each state permitting a Plaintiff in a suit to ask his opposing party, to produce documents and other information in its possession, necessary to establish that proof. Then, a Judge had great power to restrict these requests if the jurist perceives them to be burdensome. This is not so much the case today.

Although many people know me as the General Counsel of Weirton Steel Corporation from 1985 to 2004 or for almost all of its existence, before that I was in private practice for over ten years and did a fair amount of Plaintiff's litigation, including cases on behalf of persons injured in the explosion. In our cases much of what we requested was denied as either not in existence, privileged, or burdensome. In the end we received only about 150-200 of the thousands of drawings produced for the project, but we did get a number of the one's concerning the pre-heater. To understand the pre-heater we requested an operating manual and were told than none existed that was relevant to the case.

GLORY BE TO THE POWER OF THE INTERNET. While to this day, I have never found a Koppers coke oven operating manual, I have found one published in the 1970's by their prime competitor the Wilputte Corporation. Here is what Wilputte had to say about preheaters:

"Accurate (operation) requires a constant temperature gas free of any condensates. A fuel gas preheater is provided which automatically raises the temperature of incoming gas to well above the dew point, usually 115-135 degrees Fahrenheit, such that no condensate occurs in the metering devices in the small piping downstream. This unit delivers a constant temperature flow of gas through a seal pot.

Operators should open the drain once per shift to assure there is no buildup of condensates to the preheater due to a blocked line to the seal pot." (Source: Operating Instructions for Wilputte Coke Ovens, Wilputte Bulletin 7871, July 15, 1977.)

Looking back on the evidence and exhibits that we had, it was obvious that at the time of the explosion the drain lines on the pre-heater were in an open position. Indeed, the preheater had been washed down. The wash water and any condensates were drained out and the drain lines were left open.

The Wilputte instruction manual makes reference to preheater drain lines ending in a seal pot. The engineering drawings showed seal pots all over the Browns Island Battery.

Now for this to make sense I must introduce a science lesson. Gas is moved through pipes to a burner tip. Gas is under pressure. At any point where gas can escape having a reservoir of water against that opening keeps the gas from escaping. A seal pot accomplishes this purpose. It is nothing more than a water barrel that is enclosed, and into which the drain lines should have run, with the lines going beneath the level of the water. The beauty is that the barrel has a continuous feed of water on one side say at 20 inches above the ground. On the other side the barrel has a drain at say 18 inches above the ground. As long as water is running out of the drain side that means that 18 inches of water pressure is holding back the escape of gas. I think that the engineering drawings showed a line-up of 20-25 boxes labeled "seal pots" lined up in the area. All of them had gas lines entering. It was easy to trace gas lines to a "seal pot" on the drawing; EXCEPT that, on maybe my 500th review of the drawings I finally noticed that one box was not labeled "seal pot." Rather that one box to where the drain lines from the preheater emptied was labeled "SEAL PIT."

Aftermath

That one letter made all the difference in the world. There was no POT just an open PIT and since it was an open pit, there was no seal. Having looked at the drawings hundreds of times before I saw it, I am sure that all of the other approvers of the drawing in their monotonous checkouts missed it.

That miss in the drawings led to the construction of lines ending in a pit, when all of the engineers and designers believed that the lines ended in a pot. Testimony indicated that the pit was just a rubbish pit full of coffee cups, lunch bags and the other plant detritus.

*Above. Arrowhead and ceramic pieces from Brown's Island.
Bob Brandt collection. Photos by Eric Brandt.*

Photo of Logan impersonator, Dan Rucker. Taken at Fort Steuben, Steubenville, Ohio. Photo by Janet Knox

Chapter Twelve

A TALE FROM TWO BOBS

Rough sketches by Bob Brandt of implements on Brown's Island

Returning to the past, we begin again with Bob Brandt. As Bob visits the library, he brings items in. At first, he draws rough sketches of artifacts he retrieved from the island. The sample below makes no sense to us. Bit by bit, he offers more information.

What are these artifacts, and how do they involve some of the earliest settlers in the area? As Bob's trust grows, he reveals more. He shows us stones and arrowheads. Even before the intriguing mounds were built, the Ohio Valley had significance. Without written records before 1750, the archeologists help answer how long-ago people lived on the island. They tell us that humans

Secrets in the Mist

lived within twenty miles of Brown's Island about 16,000 years ago after the Ice Ages. This was not a time of constant glaciers and frigid air, but seventeen cycles of cold, then warmer air when the ice pack melted.

During the last Ice Age, huge mammals roamed the area, including the woolly mammoth, giant ground sloth, mastodon, and woodland muskox. At that time, a giant beaver would have stood taller than waist-high of a man or the size of a current black bear. According to Rodney Bartgis, a naturalist from West Virginia, "We had the short-faced bear, which is the biggest bear that's ever been known to live in North America."

The 16,000-year-old site at Meadowcroft Shelter, near Avella, Pennsylvania, lies about twenty miles from Brown's Island. It began its ascent to fame when farmer Albert Miller tripped over a groundhog hole and saw some unusual-looking artifacts. When Dr. James Adovisio , an anthropologist from the University of Pittsburgh, visited the Miller land in 1973, he found a sizable sheltered rock offering a simple place for visitors to stop and have some protection. When first encountering the site in June 1973, the new visitors found a hash pipe and some beer bottles. Digging deeper into the layers, they discovered colonial beer bottles. Their excavation lasted twenty-seven years and netted over two million artifacts, which included both plant and animal samples.

The diggers named one arrowhead after the farmer Albert Miller and realized the importance of the artifact he unearthed. It differed from previous ancient points and measured about three inches in length. With newer improvements in carbon dating, a procedure that determines the age of charcoal from fires, bones, and ceramic pieces, the arrowhead proved to be 16,000 years old.

These points belonged to the earliest peoples in the Ohio

A Tale from Two Bobs

Valley named Paleo or Ancient Native Americans. Even closer than Avella is an archaeological find in Follansbee, WV.

"Interestingly enough, Dr. Bernal Weimer, a biologist at Bethany College, possesses the femur of a mastodon found near Follansbee, West Virginia. The bone has a healed-over scar that may have been just such a spear point," Clifford Lewis writes in a 1958 West Virginia Archeologist Publication. As weather turned warmer and hunting increased, the massive animals disappeared.

New broader and notched arrowheads marked the Archaic Period that lasted from 8000 BC to 1000 BC. This design suited changes in area animals. Also, the Native Indians began using stone pots.

Bear, deer, elk, and small mammals replaced the huge animals from the prehistoric period. Bob Maslowski, originally from Weirton and now working for Marshall University, reports that deer provided 70 to 90 percent of the meat eaten by these Early Archaic Native Americans. In an article from the *West Virginia Encyclopedia*, he said these Native Americans began gathering foods, such as berries, nuts, and seeds. With global warming, rich forests developed. This gave rise to the growth of various types of trees: white pine, hemlock, oaks, sugar maple, hickory, chestnut, beech, black walnut, elm, locust, sour and sugar gum, black cherry, ash, willow, alder, birch, and sycamore. These trees formed canopies and extended to the river borders.

The Middle Archaic Period found the Native Americans relying even more on plant foods, as indicated by the discovery of nutting stones (stones that had indentations to crack nuts) and mortar and pestles. Points on spears became specific to certain regions. By 1000 BC, the bow and arrow replaced the spears.

During the late Archaic Period (3000-1000 BC), the Native

Americans relied more on Ohio River resources such as freshwater mussel shells. Mounds of discarded mussel shells, called middens, have been found on bluffs overlooking the Ohio River in the northern panhandle of West Virginia. Because this is the only place they exist in West Virginia, they are archeologically significant. One midden north of New Cumberland, West Virginia, named Globe Hill, was two miles long. Another shell site close to Browns Island was the East Steubenville site near the Market Street Bridge that crosses from the Steubenville, Ohio into Follansbee, West Virginia. Archeologists found freshwater mussels and remains of frogs and turtles on the high ridges above the West Virginia side of the Ohio River. Once the inhabitants ate the turtles, they used the shells as tools. These two digs also contained bone tools and human remains.

After the Archaic Period, the Native Americans mainly ate deer, elk, bear, squirrel, wild turkey, grouse, quail, and wild pigeons. Other small animals that provided sources of food, were raccoons, skunks, and hares. The animals also provided skins, greases, and horns for tools and ornamentation. The rivers and streams offered trout, perch, pike, catfish, sturgeon, turtles, eels, and shellfish. The Native Americans increased their numbers in this period, and plant cultivation began. This time became known as the Woodland Period, a time when more pots were introduced, and pipes made of stone or pottery were originated.

The Adena culture, famous for moundbuilding, was part of the Woodland Period. The Woodland Period started in 1000 BC and ended around 1200 A.D. During the Early-Middle Adena period, the Native Americans built circular houses with a single post in the middle. They had small mounds with few artifacts. Culturally, copper artifacts and mica came into use at this time.

The Corps of Engineers prepared a report to determine the

effects of the Ohio River Navigation system's continued use on its cultural resources. It stated, "Late Adena has been characterized by the development of complex ceremonies including large conical mounds, sacred circles, and earthworks sometimes containing settlements." Two to five houses constituted a settlement.:

Grave contents held not only human remains but also possessions of the people, such as their jewelry. Some of the copper items that were found came from a distance, indicating these people traded with others.

As I wrote my first article on Brown's Island, I was told there was a mound on Brown's Island, and the person told me their class went for a visit to the mound. I began to question this story years later when I tried to verify the mound's existence on this book's island. I ran into trouble. Mary Zwierzchowzski and I visited a few museums in the area to find answers. The largest mound in West Virginia lies 40 miles south of Weirton in Moundsville at The Grave Creek Archaeological Complex. Workers there manage the mound. The Delf Nerona Museum next to the mound serves as the state's *archaeological headquarters. They* did not have any records of a mound on Brown's Island but did have a small collection of artifacts from the island. That did not stop me from trying to find further detail on this mound.

Several mounds have been found near Brown's Island. Several were found in the Half Moon Area, which has been described as an early "garbage dump."

When Bob Brandt of Steubenville, Ohio, worked on Brown's Island before the coke ovens' construction, he discovered some tools and artifacts introduced in the Woodland Period. Without knowledge of Native American history and its earliest tools and weapons, a historian would be challenged to try to guess the purpose of some of these implements. The cruder the item, the older it could be

As the hunters made adaptations, archaeologists believe they slowly changed into the mound builders, possibly picking up the practice of building burial mounds from people to the South. The recorded Adena mounds in West Virginia numbered four hundred and twenty-four. Ohio had even more at about one thousand mounds.

The closest mounds to Brown's Island were discovered in what is now known as the Half Moon area. At the time of digs, it would have been the Patterson farm. This area is part of Weirton, West Virginia, north of the Veterans Memorial Bridge linking West Virginia and Ohio. The land included five hundred acres of bottomland. This particular location first attracted people from prehistoric times. Later, it lured Native Americans and then white settlers. Evidence of both hunters and shellfish consumers remained in the area. In the summer of 1940, Mr. Elmer Fetzer of Weirton excavated the site and sent his notes to Mr. Mayer-Oakes, an archeologist at the Carnegie Museum in Pittsburgh, Pennsylvania.

The first terrace held four mounds. Because of its size (6 feet high and 60 feet in diameter), Mound 2 caught an explorer's eye before the other smaller mounds. Fetzer, however, concentrated on Mound 1 (30 inches high and 44 feet in diameter) with no signs of previous excavation in one of his reports. This analysis lists items found in local mounds near Brown's Island.

The site had a slight natural slope, a probable reason the builders chose the area. About ten feet south of the highest point of the mound, Fetzer found a clay mixture. This hard clay covered the inner or primary mound. Dark soil, mixed with charcoal, ash, tiny fragments of burned bone, and red ochre composed the second layer. Further digging exposed a circular area of six feet in circumference. At the bottom of the three-foot-deep pit, he found a badly decomposed human skeleton in a layer of sand. He recovered a lower leg portion, enamel caps of twelve teeth, and part of a breastbone. Two hundred and fifty-two copper beads lay next to the skeleton, which Fetzer determined to be a person about five foot six inches in height.

Mr. Mayer-Oaks interpreted the materials. He believed Archaic Native Americans were hunters who came first. They left artifacts consisting of heavy stone tools and spear points. Most of the artifacts came from the late Adena period.

This brings up the question asked earlier in Chapter 1. Was there a burial mound on Browns Island? From the research provided so far, no recorded proof of a mound on the island exists. I was unable to solve the mystery of the Native American graveyard. I heard of a person in Toronto, Ohio, who supposedly possessed an old map with a mark and writing indicating a Shawnee burial ground. The person who had this map passed away, and I was unable to locate the remaining family members.

I talked to Rodney John, an employment consultant for the Council of Three Rivers American Indian Center in Pittsburgh.

Mr. John, a Native American himself, said he did not know of such a burial ground. He said, "I only knew of a couple of cases where situations such as this could be found to have adequate documentation." He added that the Native Americans did not believe in digging up bones and studying graveyard contents. I called the Shawnee Nation in Oklahoma, but they did not return my call.

Finally, after about six hundred years, the Adena people didn't just disappear but evolved into the Native Americans most familiar to us. A period of protohistory occurred in the period from A.D. 1050 AD to 1635. The Monongahela River Valley Native Americans settled in three states; they lived in the southwestern corner of Pennsylvania, Eastern Ohio, and the northern parts of West Virginia.

The Monongahela Culture grew maize and lived in palisaded villages with up to fifty to a hundred structures. The dwellings stood inside the barricade, and the center contained an oval plaza.

As the explorers started coming to the area, they found tribal Native Americans. This set up the stage for all sides claiming the land as their own and ensuing battles.

A Place to Visit

Grave Creek Mound Archaelogical Complex

The Grave Creek Mound in Moundsville, West Virginia is outside the Complex and is over 2000 years old. Its large conical size draws visitors. Adjacent to the mound is the Delf Nerona Museum. Inside are displays and exhibits detailing the life of the Adena people. The U.S. Corps of Engineers gave the Museum 450,000 artifacts that they recovered in the Kanawha Valley which covered 10,000 years of human habitation. The museum has some artifacts from Brown's Island, although they are not out for display. They have a canoe used by early Native Americans.

The Adena people built the mound over a period of a hundred years. They carried the dirt in baskets, and it totaled close to 60,000 tons of soil. The Complex offers special events throughout the year as well as being open to the public Tuesday through Saturday.

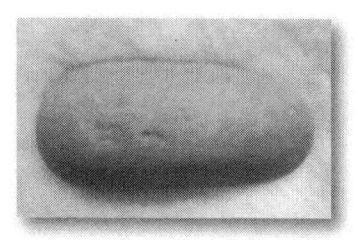

Grinding Stone Above. Celt below. From Bob Brandt collection. Taken by Eric Brandt.

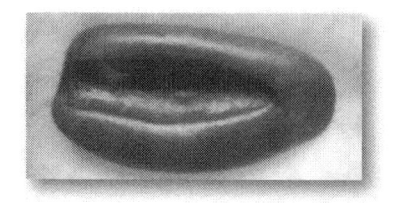

Fishing line sinkers. From Bob Brandt collection. Taken by Eric Brandt.

Secrets in the Mist

*Arrowheads found on Browns Island by Bob Brandt.
Photo by Eric Brandt*

Chapter Thirteen

TRIBAL INDIANS AND EXPLORERS

As interest in the Ohio Valley grew and Europeans ventured down the Ohio River, some newer boat types entered the waters. However, canoes still dominated the rivers. The Native tribes relied on the canoe using a heavy canoe and a lighter version. The weightier canoe was known as a "dugout" or "pirogue" in the south. The Native Americans carved the dugout from a tree and stripped the bark away. They shaped and hollowed the canoe using an ax or "adze", sometimes burning the inside to waterproof the canoe. This strong boat could navigate rapids and shallows. The Native Americans built the other canoe from lighter wood, usually birch, setting it around a thin frame. A single person could lift this canoe. Even though small, it transported large loads. Explorers and traders often favored this type of boat.

Canoes suited this area for centuries because the Native Americans mainly made short trips to hunting grounds or crossed the river with supplies. The settlers in the area also used canoes until after the Lewis and Clark Expedition when the larger migration of Easterners required hardier boats.

By the time European explorers brought their boats down the Ohio River to the Northern Panhandle of West Virginia, they had viewed scant evidence of Native American settlements. Where had these native people gone? Although it seemed as the Adena and Monongahela had disappeared, some of them had evolved, moved, and banded together in groups or tribes as a means of protection. They also died from diseases brought by the white men and from fatal conflicts among the Indians themselves.

The epidemics and diseases from the French settlers killed many Native Americans. A smallpox epidemic also wiped out half the Iroquois population to the North. The Native Americans had a remarkable trait of having no traces of familiar diseases such as the flu and even the common cold. Scientists theorized this was due to their travels across the Bering land bridge. The sick and weakened on the trip could not withstand the frigid cold and died on the way. This left the ones that survived with little exposure to disease. Archaeologists studied mummified Native Americans (either on purpose or for some other reason), and found them susceptible to cancer and arthritis, but rarely to tooth decay. The Paleo-Indians died through battle, accidents, and starvation but not often from sickness. Simple items like a blanket could pass the smallpox disease to their susceptible descendants. One other reason the tribes perished was due to climate events such as droughts that left them with little food. They died from starvation.

The Ohio Valley was mainly used for hunting and the Ohio River for launching battles. Hunting trips at that time were for much longer duration than the hunting done today. During the 1600s, many tribes left the northern Ohio River's land due to the Beaver Wars. In these wars, the Iroquois fought with other tribes to gain access to the land and territories known as the Ohio Country. They wished to control the area where new beavers would be found. The French considered the beaver a valued trade item, proving lucrative to the Native Americans who hunted the beaver.

Tribal Indians and Explorers

The Iroquois domination was one reason few Native Americans lived in West Virginia and the Ohio side of the river in the upper Ohio Valley. Some of the Native Americas who did settle in Ohio, such as the Miami, moved to the Scioto River in the Columbus area of Ohio. The Iroquois Confederacy began when five tribes of Upper New York joined together: the Mohawk, Cayuga, Oneida, Onondaga, and Seneca people. This made them a powerful group. Eventually, they added the Tuscarora and were renamed the Six Tribes. Although they did not settle in the Ohio Valley, they had control of the area. They bought firearms from the Dutch. They believed their unity of tribes made them great and authoritative. Other tribes saw them as arrogant. Their center was Niagara Falls (Onondaga), and they considered an assault on any of the tribes as an insult to all the Iroquois.

One of the tribes the European travelers did see was the Shawnee, who became formidable and a threat to the Iroquois. Before the colonists entered the picture, the Shawnee numbered around 10,000. By the war of 1812, only about 3500 of the tribe lived in America. The Shawnee, a highly mobile group, moved to avoid engaging in conflicts and to follow the food supply. Because of their constant traveling, they lived in wigwams, round in shape similar to igloos. Tree saplings provided the pole framework structure covered with bark sheets from trees and other natural materials.

The Mingo had small settlements in the upper Ohio Valley. Mingo was not an actual tribe but a meld of the Seneca-Cayuga Indians. One important Mingo was Logan, also known as Talgayeeta. Logan's father knew William Penn and, through him, John Logan, Penn's provincial secretary for the Pennsylvania Colony. He respected both Penn and John Logan, and when his son was born in 1731, the Cayuga chief gave his son a secondary name of Logan. Logan lived in Pennsylvania but eventually moved to

Ohio at the Mingo townsite (Mingo Junction). The Delaware had originally inhabited this area, but the Mingo renamed the site after settling there. The Delaware, Mingo-Iroquois, and the Shawnee started to live in harmony and started mixing and living on the same lands. They were all fishermen, so the Ohio River gave them a great source for fish and crawdads. Logan next moved to Yellow Creek, close to where a rest stop exists on Ohio State 7. He would play a prominent role in the hostilities that developed in the Ohio River Valley.

The Delaware, or Lenape (meaning The People), also ended up on the Ohio frontier. Their important Algonquian Confederacy numbered about 11,000 in 1600. They had people on the coast of the Atlantic and the Delaware River Basin and were the first to interact with the Europeans, originally with the Dutch and Swedes and then the English.

The French explorers came first with Robert La Salle, born in France in 1643 and trained for the priesthood. At 22, LaSalle set forth for Canada, where he farmed the land and set up a trading post in Montreal. In 1669, he headed southwestward and claimed to have found the Ohio River, which he followed to Louisville. In many places, La Salle is credited as the first European to view the Ohio River, but modern historians believe that his claim may not be accurate.

In 1682, he did make it to the Mississippi River and proceeded to the Gulf of Mexico. He said all the territories on the Ohio and Mississippi now belonged to France, and he called it Louisiana. In 1684, he tried to establish a colony at the mouth of the Mississippi. In 1687, the French King, Louis XIV, wanted him to conquer a part of Mexico, as France and Spain were at odds. He ended up in Texas, where some of his men mutinied and killed him.

Another French explorer was Celeron de Blainville (also referred to as Bienville), born in Montreal in 1693. He became a cadet in the colonial regulars of Canada at the age of 13. He was promoted to first ensign in 1715, and by 1738, he obtained the position of captain. In June of 1749, he left Montreal with 213 men made up of regulars, militia, and a few Indians. Large boats and canoes comprised the flotilla that left Niagara to Lake Erie. Following the south shore of Lake Erie, he travelled south to the Allegheny River, burying the first of a series of lead plates along the way to mark France's land. In West Virginia, he buried four plaques, the closest one buried at Wheeling Creek. This plate has never been found. Several boys at Point Pleasant found one of the plates and turned it into a hotel's proprietor at Point Pleasant. Ultimately, the plate was presented to the Virginia Historical Society for validation. The last plate was buried at the mouth of the Ohio in Cincinnati.

As he came down the Ohio River, he met English traders whom he ordered to leave. He also noticed groups of Indians from the Mingo, Shawnee, and Miami tribes who appeared friendly towards the British. After five months, he returned from his three-thousand-mile trip in the unmapped hostile territory. He only lost one man on his journey. His reports recommended that a road be built with military fortifications, and he noted it would be costly to build. He also encouraged thousands of French immigrants to come over and settle there.

English explorers

A group of colonists departed from Petersburg, Virginia, in 1761 to explore the lands beyond the mountains. Thomas Batts, Thomas Wood, and Robert Fallam headed towards the southern part of West Virginia and are credited with discovering the New

River, then called the Wood River. Some speculated they made it to the Western part of Virginia to the Ohio River. The important part of this voyage is that it gave the English leverage in treaty negotiations after the French and Indian War.

Probably the most famous person to come down the Ohio River was George Washington. He first came to Virginia to meet the French in Logstown (now Economy, Pennsylvania). The French built cabins for the natives to live in, and the spot served as a trading center. Washington tried to get the tribal chiefs to side with the English to govern the area. He went to Fort Duquesne (present-day Fort Pitt) to order the French to leave.

After leaving Mt. Vernon on October 5, 1770, Washington arrived in Pittsburgh on October 15. He embarked on a canoe trip to inspect lands for claims. Washington passed by Yellow Creek and Brown's Island on October 22. He described it as the long island (which tho so distinguished is not very remarkable for length, breadth or goodness). He mentioned a creek that comes in on the east side of the River, "the name of which I could not learn." The creek he described is King's Creek in northern Weirton. He then mentions Mingo Town, now known as Mingo Junction, on the west side of the river. Washington stated there were about twenty cabins and seventy Native Americans at this location. Visitors can see a marker for his crossing on Route 2 in Brooke County near Wellsburg, West Virginia.

Crossing sign close to Wellsburg, West Virginia

Facsimile of Celeron Plate displayed at Ohio County Public Library. Photo by Jane Kraina

Chapter Fourteen

WARS, ATTACKS, AND CAPTURES

The series of wars and attacks that began in 1754 changed the Upper Ohio Valley's unsettled area to a land usurped from the Native Americans and the French. The eventual winners of the land were first the English and then the settlers from the newly founded United States. Three forces had reasons to fight over the Ohio Valley. The Native Americans wanted to maintain their land for the present and the future. They wished to trade with the French and English but opposed both European groups settling there. Both the French and British claimed the land. All the conflicts in the area would affect the future of Brown's Island.

The French had claimed the land for New France, which already had settlements in Canada, Louisiana, and Illinois. The Ohio River acted as a communication conduit for the French. They weren't eager to set up settlements in the Upper Ohio Valley, however, they desired open movement for priests and traders. Marquis Duquesne took the governorship of New France in 1752, and it was his responsibility to keep the British out of the area. The French began building forts and trading posts. At this time, New France had 70,000 settlers.

The British believed they owned the Ohio Valley due to

Wars, Attacks, and Captures

Virginia's charter that granted land clear to the Pacific Ocean (Manifest Destiny). The British also traded with the Native Americans, but their primary interest was farming, the center of their economy. They also sought the use of the Ohio River as a navigable route. The French who were active in the area thwarted their plans. The British had the largest population of settlers of the two countries with one million newcomers in the colonies.

The Native Americans had recently moved to the Northern Panhandle area of West Virginia and eastern Ohio; some had only been there for about thirty years. Because they numbered three to four thousand in the area, they had the most to lose. Both European groups threatened their way of life and the land that provided their food. The British and the French curried their favor by giving them gifts, including guns, gunpowder, and household items. These offerings were about the only gain for the natives from contact with the new presences in the area.

The French and Indian War fought in North America was part of a world conflict between Britain France to establish dominance lasting from 1754-1763. Although the war swirled around the northern panhandle of West Virginia and southeastern Ohio, most of the conflicts occurred around Pittsburgh, Pennsylvania and southern Virginia. The Native Americans sided with the French because the British posed a more significant threat of taking the Native Americans' land. In 1753, George Washington, (then colonel of the Virginia Militia) came to Pittsburgh to warn the French to get out of the area. The British took over the French Fort Duquesne in Pittsburgh, Pennsylvania. As the French left, they burned the fort. From 1759 to 1761, the British rebuilt the fort and renamed it Fort Pitt.

Although the British had been cautioned that their formal fighting style would not be successful against the guerrilla warfare common on the frontier, they still won the war. The Native Americans were quite surprised that war treaties could be signed across the ocean in Europe and not in the colonies where the fighting had occurred. The French and Indian War did not settle the hostilities occurring in the Western "Frontier" as more land-hungry colonists crossed the Allegheny Mountains. King George III of Britain issued the Royal Proclamation of 1763, declaring the land west of the Continental Divide to serve as a Native American Reserve and that the settlers in the Ohio River Valley should vacate and move back to the East. The British colonists then renegotiated with the Native Americans and permitted them to inhabit the land in Ohio and westwards.

Local attacks continued with both sides targeting individuals and families. One killing that took place involved island petroglyphs (figures "developed by sculpturing—carving, pecking, rubbing or a combination of these techniques). From 1950 and 1956, a program directed by William Mayer-Oakes decided the northern part of West Virginia and the western part of Pennsylvania deserved more study. This study was dubbed the Upper Ohio Valley Archeological Survey. Scientists explored the sites and carbon-dated relics to determine their age. At a hearth site on Brown's Island, they found a Watson Ware ceramic fragment and a Watson elbow pipe. These had come from a farm owned by Watson nearby. Chemists from the Carnegie Institute of Technology, who carbon-dated the charcoal from the old fire site, determined the date of the charcoal at 1200 AD, with a leeway of one hundred years. The Watson site artifacts dated as far back as 500 BC.

James Swauger, a participant in the study above, wrote a book detailing the petroglyphs found at Browns Island. Harold Barth had a collection of tracings of the rocks, photographs, and notes about petroglyphs around the East Liverpool, Ohio area. He noted the Native Americans carved them in sandstone. In the *History of*

Jefferson County, the author included a photograph of two sandhill cranes. Most of the 47 designs were of animals, but some portrayed mythological creatures. James Swauger concluded that the rock art designs were carved by Algonquian-tongued Monongahela Man groups, proto-Shawnee, sometime between 1200 and 1750 BC.

Archeologist Stanley Baker of Ohio wrote more about the petroglyphs in an article published in 2011 recording early observations of these rock pictures. James Barton wrote of the petroglyphs in 1799. Next, Mcbride wrote of his visit to the area in 1838. Charles Whittlesey thought the petroglyphs resembled pictographs (painted artwork rather than carved) of recent natives. He recorded that Jacob Myers, an Indian Scout and early settler around Toronto, Ohio, shot an Indian in 1774, and a local paper published the account of Myers. Myers was on the then Virginia shore, and when he rafted over to the island, he saw that the Native American was working on the rock. Myers lived to be 107, and his grave lies at the Toronto Union Cemetery in Toronto, Ohio. The name on the grave is Auvrel Myers, but he was known as "Mike." The keepers of the books for the Toronto Union Cemetery said it was common in those times for settlers to change their names. These rocks are no longer visible and probably disappeared when the water deepened while putting in dams and locks. Publications fall into two schools of thought: one that the petroglyphs lay on the island and another that they existed on the West Virginia shore. Recordings of these figures lie in about a thirty-mile area from Pennsylvania to West Virginia.

With tensions running high between the settlers and the Native Americans, white settlers in the area met in Wheeling, West Virginia (then Virginia). Their talks reflected differing opinions. George Rogers Clark, Jacob Greathouse, and Michael Cresap favored killing Native American parties, while Ebenezer Zane and his family thought outright murder would provoke war.

Cresap rounded up a party of thirty men and killed three Indians at Captina Creek's mouth in Belmont County, Ohio.

Settlers began leaving the Wheeling area, fearing retribution from the Native Americans. They took a different route other than the Ohio River, not wanting to be an easy target. Cresap, influenced by Jacob Greathouse, planned to attack the village of Talgayeeta at Yellow Creek, where Logan lived. Daniel Greathouse, a scout from Newell, West Virginia and brother to Jacob, joined the party to lure the Mingoes over to the Virginia side of the river. At this point, Cresap had second thoughts about hurting Logan, who showed friendship toward the whites. So, the party now had the Greathouse brothers and James King.

Jacob and Daniel traveled by canoe to the Mingo camp, offering drink and shooting contests. Logan was not at the encampment, but his brother was. Logan's father, brother, sister (who was late in her pregnancy), and her young daughter joined two others to meet the white camp at Baker's Tavern (in the area of the present-day Mountaineer Casino, Racetrack, and Resort). In April of 1774, the Greathouse party shot the Native Americans, sparing only the little girl, whose supposed father was John Gibson, a white man. When Logan learned of the murder of his family, he retaliated against the white settlers in the area. In *The History of Hancock County, Virginia and West Virginia* by Jack Welch, he wrote, "When the chief learned that his father, mother, and sister had been killed, he became incensed with grief and vowed that the whites would pay ten scalps for one. That very summer Logan is reported to have fulfilled his vow by taking thirty white scalps with his own knife."

After these revenge killings and subsequent attacks from the Mingoes and Shawnees, Lord Dunmore, governor of Virginia, decided to subdue the Shawnees. The conflict was called

Wars, Attacks, and Captures

Dunmore's War. He commanded about a thousand men to go to the mouth of the Hocking River in Ohio. Meanwhile, another militia unit led by Colonel Andrew Lewis gathered in Lewisburg, West Virginia, and proceeded to the Kanawha River's mouth in Point Pleasant, West Virginia. This group defeated the Shawnees led by Cornstalk in the Battle of Point Pleasant. When Lord Dunmore learned of this victory, he settled with the Shawnees, giving them back prisoners, horses, and property. In exchange, the Shawnees agreed to stop hunting south of the Ohio River.

Lord Dunmore was not a popular man, and military leaders were disturbed that he stalled the start of the American Revolution. The revolutionary battles fought in this area repeated the guerrilla types of attacks the frontiersmen had encountered in earlier wars. The closest battle location to Brown's Island occurred at the Wheeling fortification named Fort Henry. Robert Kaminski of Weirton wrote in a *Weirton Daily Times Bicentennial Issue* article about a 1777 attack, "On Sept. 1, Simon Girty an American Army deserter and white renegade fighting for the British, led a full-scale attack of over 300 Indians on Fort Henry in Wheeling."

The families who took cover there fought back, but the Native Americans kept persisting. Kaminski adds, "Colonel Andrew Swearingen and John Schoolcraft led a small force from the blockhouse in Hollidays Cove (now Weirton) located approximately at a site across from the present Kentucky Fried Chicken Restaurant." This small group gave the Wheeling settlers some relief until more local forces could arrive.

Frontier scouts warned Wheeling about the next attack in 1781, so the residents could fight back. The battle continued in Ohio between the Native American settlements located between Zanesville and Coshocton on the Muskingum River. Finally, Fort Henry served as the last battle of the revolution. The British moved in with about three hundred Indians and played their drums and fifes. The defenders in Wheeling numbered about 58, but as brave Betty Zane ran to get more gunpowder for the settlers, the English and Indians retreated.

Although the wars stopped, skirmishes continued, and the settlers had to build forts and prepare for attacks as the Native Americans persisted into the 1790s. Forts in the area close to Brown's Island were Croxton's Stone Blockhouse in Toronto, Ohio; Chapman's Blockhouse in New Cumberland, West Virginia; Griffith's Stone Blockhouse, Holliday's Cove Fort; and Edgington's Fort in Weirton. Fort Steuben (an outpost for land surveyors) lay in Steubenville, Fort Decker in Follansbee, and Sappington Fort near the current Brooke-Hancock County line. Richard Wells' Blockhouse in Mingo's Bottom, Ohio, McGuire's Fort, Cox's Blockhouse in Wellsburg, West Virginia all sat close to Cross Creek.

The Edgington family had intriguing experiences in the area. George Edgington initially moved to Hampshire County, West Virginia in the vicinity of Dillon's Run. George and his wife Margaret had eight children. The boys were Thomas, John, Jesse, Joseph, Isaac, and George Jr. The two girls were Jemima and Hannah. A relative of Edgington writes about George's experience with the Native Americans at the beginning of the French and Indian War: "Early on, George was captured not far from his home by French-sympathizing Indians who took him to Fort Duquesne... From there, George was taken up the Scioto River, where he was kept for three years. He would eventually return home in 1757."

Several Edgington family members would move to Hollidays Cove, and some would be involved with Brown's Island. Thomas, the eldest son, moved to western Pennsylvania in 1771. He first came to Redstone Fort on the Nemacolin Trail in Pennsylvania, close to Brownsville. He met Andrew Van Swearingen, who sold him seven hundred acres of land near Washington, Pennsylvania. Edgington moved his family there first, but as forts sprung up to defend the land along the upper Ohio River, Thomas moved to Holliday's Cove, Virginia now Weirton, West Virginia.

In 1779, Thomas became part of an elite group of men known as "Brady's Rangers." They patrolled the area and warned the settlers of impending attacks. At 35 years of age, Thomas was the oldest member of the group led by Samuel Brady.

Thomas and his family moved to Holliday's Cove, traveling the Ohio River on a giant raft or flatboat. Edgington commissioned workers to build the raft in Sawmill Run, Pennsylvania. This boat carried his whole family, along with livestock, and all the family's possessions. When the family reached their settlement, they would disassemble the raft. The logs would then be repurposed to build their home. When neighbors came to help him build his cabin, they told him of attacks from the Native Americans, so Thomas also built a fort on his property close to where Harmon's Creek flowed into the Ohio River. Eventually, Thomas and all his brothers joined the Pennsylvania Militia and served in James Munn's Company, 2nd Battalion, Washington County.

In 1782, like his father before him, Thomas was captured by a group of Native Americans. "In April 1782, while barely a mile from his home near Holliday's Cove, Thomas was captured by a party of nine Wyandot Indians who were accompanied [by] Simon Girty, a former British interpreter who had defected from Fort Pitt. Thomas knew Girty, which may have led his Indian captors to treat him less harshly during his captivity." In the spring of 1783, he returned to his home. His family had moved back to their old home in Washington, and Thomas found them and brought them back to Holliday's Cove. Around 1783, Thomas's father, mother, and sister lived on the property that Thomas had claimed. His father, George, died there in 1784.

Isaac and Joseph, brothers of Thomas, settled on Hart's Rock on Brown's Island at the island's northern tip. They built cabins there for their families. However, members of Congress had told them they could not live there, as they had not purchased the land. Subsequently the federal government backed up their threat by burning down their cabins. They were the first white men that lived on the island. After they were ousted from the island, they settled elsewhere, Isaac in Washington County, Pennsylvania and Joseph in Ohio.

Another family story involved George (Thomas's son). He was on Browns Island and discovered the skeleton of a Native American who had been shot dead from a canoe at Montour's Run. He had drifted downstream twenty-seven miles from the skirmish. George reported the body, and his father said he could keep the skull. "It was still a grisly memento in the George Edgington household, when he was 92 years old in 1860, the bullet hole clearly evident."

Several families were massacred on the Ohio side of the river. An Indian attack party killed members of the Riley family in Salt Run in 1792. As the family worked on their field, the Native Americans killed the father, mother, and younger son. The older son hid in the bushes, and the attackers captured the family's two girls. About half a mile west of New Alexandria, the Native Americans tomahawked one of the sisters. The other girl, a captive of the Indians, lived with the Indians. Her older brother, James Riley, located her years later, but she wished to stay with the Indians she considered family.

Wars, Attacks, and Captures

Indians in Chester County, Pennsylvania took Mary Jemison, 13, after killing her parents. They gave her to two Seneca squaws at Ft. Duquesne. She passed Brown's Island. According to records from the Jefferson County Historical Society, "The Senecas took Mary with them in a canoe they set out on the river for Mingo town. As they drifted down the river, they passed a Shawnee town where Northern Jefferson County is now located. Mary trembled as she saw the remains of white men who had been tortured and burned. Their bodies were supported in forked poles, suspended above the fire. Mary was adopted by the Senecas and married an Indian chief. She lived as an Indian until her death at age 90 in 1833."

By 1795, the last person to be killed in Brooke County was John Decker, who was attacked by the Wyandots. They tomahawked and scalped him. By the 1800s, people began tearing down their forts or rebuilding them as part of their family homes.

Chapter Fifteen

LEWIS AND CLARK VISIT THE ISLAND

President Thomas Jefferson envisioned exploring the northwestern part of the continent for twenty years before putting his dreams into reality. At the beginning of 1803, two years into his presidential term, he had sufficient power to obtain backing for the venture. He asked Congress to fund a military trip to learn more about the United States' western region. The budget for the journey was $2500. In January, this land did not belong to the United States but to the French. Napoleon Bonaparte sold approximately 827,000 acres to the United States in the Louisiana Purchase signed in May of 1803, transferring the land to the United States at the cost of three to four cents an acre, an unbelievable real estate deal.

President Jefferson chose Meriwether Lewis to lead the expedition. Meriwether's father, William Lewis (who died when Meriwether was five), had known Jefferson. Their farms had been relatively close in Virginia, and Jefferson's siblings married into the Lewis family. Jefferson also knew the Meriwether family and was familiar with Lucy Meriwether, who married Lt. William Lewis. The Lewis side of the family had a melancholic trait, which Meriwether exhibited. Meriwether's mother taught him about herbs and botany, lessons which proved valuable on his trip. Jefferson chose Lewis as his personal secretary because of the trusted family connections and Meriwether's knowledge of the western territory.

Meriwether possessed qualities of perseverance and steadiness. He had traversed the "Far West" frontier territory of Ohio, had served in the military, and had excelled in hunting skills. He was also familiar with Native Americans and their ways. Also, he could record the discoveries in his journey.

Meriwether Lewis wanted to leave by July 20, 1803, to start his waterway trip to explore the Missouri River and the westward-flowing streams into the Pacific Ocean. He had planned to return home by 1804; instead, he encountered glitches at the beginning of the trip.

When Jefferson put his proposal before Congress, he offered justification for the trip: to further the fur trade, to gather scientific and geographic information, and to map the area adequately. Gathering supplies for a journey of such magnitude took Meriwether four months. Because he had to learn how to observe the stars, he trained under Andrew Ellicott, who was highly skilled in astronomy and mathematics.

Supplies included food. Buying a "Portable Soup" cost the most, and it totaled close to three hundred dollars for about two hundred pounds. Meriwether also needed rifles, axes, knives, other weapons, a chronometer (an instrument for measuring time), other measuring devices, rifle powder, medicine, medical supplies, tobacco, fishing hooks, tackle, cloth, awls, and needles. He ordered whiskey, a standard military issue at the time. Lewis bought ink and paper for the journal he would be keeping. The group would replenish provisions on their trip when possible. Lewis purchased gifts for the Native Americans they would encounter, including beads, sewing items, paint, knives, and ear trinkets.

In June, Lewis decided he needed another man to help lead the group in case anything would happen. He chose William Clark, his former commanding officer. Lewis wrote him a letter. Since mail took a lot longer to reach its destination then, Meriwether arranged to have Lt. Moses Hooke as a backup. It was July 29 while Lewis was in Pittsburgh waiting for his keelboat that he heard from William Clark.

President Jefferson thought Lewis should be the supreme commander. Lewis differed, believing that they should be co-leaders, respecting that Clark had been his senior officer in the past. The government made Clark a lieutenant, but that did not stop Lewis from treating Clark as an equal in command. Clark would meet Lewis in Louisville, Kentucky.

Clark, a robust redheaded man, was born in Virginia. His older brother was George Rogers Clark, a Revolutionary War hero. William followed his brother's path into a military career. He had a hearty laugh and could lead men. He was steady, reliable, and not prone to introspection like Lewis. His talent in drawing proved valuable as he sketched wildlife and plants.

Although the famous Lewis and Clark expedition began officially in Illinois, where the Ohio River and Mississippi River joined, Meriwether had to obtain his keelboat in Pittsburgh, Pennsylvania. From there, he would travel down the Ohio River. Lewis left Washington and stopped in Frederick, Maryland, on July 5. Then he stopped in Harper's Ferry to procure his supplies, the most important being the iron frame of the collapsible boat they would use in the trip's mountainous areas. This frame weighed only forty-four pounds. Covered with hides, it could carry 1,770 pounds. While in Harper's Ferry (the U.S. Military arsenal at the time), he also tested the guns he had purchased there for the trip, some of them specifically customized for his needs.

Lewis and Clark Visit the Island

According to Meriwether Lewis, the boatbuilder in Pittsburgh had been negligent and delayed the start of the trip by six weeks. The boat builder was a drinker and kept irregular hours. Lewis also bought two pirogues (shallow flat bottom boats) to help with the heavy load they would take down the river. Sometimes sources site the boats as canoes, but they were much larger than the canoes of today's time. On August 31, 1803, Meriwether Lewis and his party left Pittsburgh to start their Ohio River journey.

Lewis bought his Newfoundland dog Seaman (referred to as Scannon in some sources) in Pittsburgh to take on his trip. The dog survived the entire trip. Early in the journey, some Indians offered three beaver skins for the dog. Lewis was insulted, as he had paid $20 for the dog. He also liked the temperament of the dog.

After only three miles down the river from Pittsburgh, Lewis stopped to show some pioneers the pneumatic rifle he had purchased in Philadelphia, Pennsylvania. The gun, powered by air, made no noise and emitted no smoke. While the pioneers were passing the gun around, it went off inadvertently, and hit a woman in the head. She dropped to the ground and bled from her temple; however, she came to and was not in any danger. That was the end of demonstrations of the gun after someone had loaded the weapon.

Because of the late start, the river was relatively low. Men from Pittsburgh had advised them not to go at that time because of the shallowness of the river. Sandbars and riffles became a problem. As he met people along the route, he got advice on some of the river's travel conditions.

Janet Knox, from Wellsburg, WV, who was related to the early Knox residents of Hollidays Cove (now part of Weirton), boated on the Ohio River and camped on Brown's Island in the 1980s. She said, "The riffles that Lewis referred to indicate shallow parts of the river and can be seen in advance. People in the front of the boat can look out for these formations in the river, which are lighter in color and somewhat diamond shaped. If you are not careful, your boat can get stuck in these areas."

Lewis observed that the people near the river made money by helping travelers. He had to pay for horses and oxen to hoist the boat over the low spots. Sometimes he found the fees to be higher than they should be. In Georgetown, Pennsylvania, above Chester, West Virginia (then Virginia), his crew bought a canoe and two paddles. The boat leaked, and they had to bail the water out constantly. The men had to air out some of the supplies as they got wet. The hauling of the boat and the constant transferring of items greatly fatigued the men.

Lewis noted that felled trees marked the state line of West Virginia (then Virginia). The downed trees measured about sixty feet in width. Around Chester, West Virginia, the water was so low and clear they could see the fish that Lewis recognized as bass, pike, sturgeon, and catfish.

He noted that the fogs in this area differed from those in other regions of the country he had traveled. The dew from the trees falling to the ground gave the impression of gentle rain.

The following entries of September 5th and 6th are from *The Journals of the Lewis and Clark Expedition,* edited by Gary Moulton and published by the Lincoln, University of Nebraska Press 1986. The entries are the spelling of Meriwether Lewis.

September 5

"Again foggey, loaded both my canoes and waited till the fogg disappeared set out at 8 OCl. had some difficulty in passing several riffles today but surmounted it without having recorse to horses or oxen— rained at six this evening and continued with some intervals through the night to rain pretty heard (hard); took up at the head of Brown's Island (1); it grew very dark and my canoes which had on board the most valuable part of my stores had not come up, ordered the trumpet to be sound and they answered.— they came up in a few minutes after; the stores in the canoes being well secured with oil cloth I concluded to let them remain on board and directed that the water which they maid should be bailed out of them occasionally through the night, which was done—they still leaked considerably notwithstanding the repairs which I had made on them; we came 16 miles this day"

> (1) chapter, is located opposite the town of Weirton, Hancock County, West Virginia. The name is from a nearby landowner of the period. Thwaites (EWT), 4:105-6.
>
> (2) Probably one of the "4 Tin blowing Trumpets" purchased in Philadelphia, which would be more convenient for signaling on this expedition than the drums and fifes used by the military at this period. Lewis' List [June 30, 1803], Jackson (LLC), 1:71, 95. On the next day, they proceeded to Steubenville, Ohio. Lewis described the thick fog, an air temperature of 71 degrees, and a water temperature of 73 degrees. After getting stuck on a riffle, they had to obtain horses to get over the sandy bottoms. Lewis complained, "the man charged the exorbitant price of two dollars for his trouble."

Again, they were stuck on a riffle, and he had to locate horses and oxen. He described Steubenville, Ohio as a small well-built thriving place with several respectable families residing in it. Only five years prior, it was a wilderness. The oxen exited off the boats with difficulty and pulled back; however, with their assistance they crossed over two more sandbars. They proceeded about a mile and a half further and encamped on the west bank of the river.

The group landed in Wheeling on September 7, 1803. In November of 1804, they arrived at the junction of the Ohio River and the Mississippi River. Lewis spent most of his time in St. Louis, trying to learn as much as he could about the lands they would soon travel. William Clark wintered at Camp Wood, Illinois and trained the men for the long expedition. The men he selected formed the Corps of Discovery. Lewis and Clark spent the time rounding up supplies and men for the trip. Both men showed sternness toward the party of men. Clark took his black servant with him, and he became a novelty to the Native Americans who had never seen a man of such dark color.

Forced to wait for winter to end, they didn't even leave for the journey up the Missouri River until mid-May of 1804. After many difficulties, the expedition was a time frame of two years, four months, and ten days. At that time, the explorers returned to St. Louis. They had traveled over eight thousand miles. Since they had not communicated with anyone since 1805, Americans speculated about what had happened to them during their trip. Some said the whole group had been killed or taken captive by Spaniards, who forced them into mining duties. Their trip achieved many milestones and some disappointments. The military leadership of Lewis proved superb. Although the Corps of Discovery found a route that settlers would use in the future, they did not find a route that could be achieved totally by waterway. The Native Americans in the western region did not recognize American rule for their territories, but the group connected with Native Americans who had never seen a white man.

The number of new plants they recorded numbered almost two hundred, and they also labeled over a hundred new animal species. Lewis reported a plentiful supply of beaver for commercial use. The methods Lewis applied in recording his discoveries served as a model for future explorers. The mountains the men encountered were beyond anything they had witnessed in the Eastern part of the country, and the trees towered much higher than ones they remembered from their homelands. Their discovery was truly phenomenal in the history of America.

Another Place to Visit

Fort Steuben, Steubenville, Ohio

The following piece comes from Paul Zuros, director of the Historic Fort Steuben.

"Fort Steuben was built in 1786 by the First American Regiment to protect surveyors tasked with surveying the first seven ranges of the newly acquired Northwest Territory on the west side of the Ohio River. After the American Revolution, the young country acquired as part of the Treaty of Paris, the land known as the Northwest Territory, today consisting of the states of Ohio, Indiana, Michigan, Illinois, Wisconsin, and parts of Minnesota.

"To raise needed funds for the government, surveyors were sent out from Fort Pitt to begin surveying the land west of the Ohio River in 1785. The surveyors were met with threats of violence from the Native Americans who were still residing in the area and shortly after beginning, the group returned to Fort Pitt until a military escort could be arranged.

"The following year in 1786, the surveyors once again returned to the Northwest Territory to continue to survey the area. This time, they were escorted by the First American Regiment who would provide military assistance if needed. Another major role of the

First American Regiment was to remove illegal settlers or squatters who had settled in the Ohio Country without a legal claim to the land. The First American Regiment would ask the settlers to leave the area, and if they did not vacate, the regiment would threaten to burn them out, which happened on a few occasions.

"By October of 1786, winter quarters were needed so the decision was made to construct a Fort near the Ohio River to pass the winter months and serve as the headquarters for the remaining surveying operations. The commander of the First American Regiment, Revolutionary War Veteran John Francis Hamtramck decided to name the fort after Revolutionary War hero Friedrich Wilhelm Augustus Heinrich Ferdinand, Baron von Steuben.

"Only after 8 months at Fort Steuben, the survey of the Seven Ranges was completed, and the army moved on. The Fort was abandoned and was gone from the landscape by 1790. The town that eventually grew up around the site of the original fort a decade later, took the name "Steubenville" in honor of the former Fort Steuben and its history.

"Over the years, many attempts were made at reconstructing the Fort even as early as the 1870s, but those were not successful. In 1986 the Old Fort Steuben Project was organized with the purpose of reconstructing the Fort. In 1989 the first block house was built on the forts original site and the other buildings followed as funding allowed. The fort was officially completed in 2009. Today Fort Steuben encompasses an entire city block in downtown Steubenville and consists of the Fort, Visitor Center, Fort Steuben Park, Fountain, Berkman Amphitheater, and the First Federal Land Office in the Northwest Territory."

Chapter Sixteen

THE BROWNS OF BROWN'S ISLAND

The year was 1776. The war for independence had begun, and Colonel Richard Brown served with honor. Born in Frederick County, Maryland in 1739, Brown fought in two wars—the French and Indian War and later the American Revolution. He earned the rank of colonel while serving with a Maryland regiment under the command of General George Washington. A few years after the Revolution ended, Col. Brown, his wife Honor and two of their three children packed up their belongings and headed west to a new frontier. They arrived in Holliday's Cove, Virginia around 1786. His brother Hugh Brown and wife Ruth, also of Maryland, would soon follow.

Shortly after they settled, Brown made several land transactions. Ohio County deed records show that on June 19, 1787, Richard Brown purchased from Moses Holaday and wife Elizabeth "one half of an island in the Ohio River known as Cove Island, jointly owned by Moses Holaday and Benjamin Johnston." Again, on September 18, 1789, Brown purchased from Benjamin Johnston "for the sum of seventy-five pounds, three hundred-and fifty-nine acres part of an island situated in the Ohio River opposite Holliday's Cove, which was granted to Benjamin Johnson and Moses Holliday." The two combined land transfers gave Brown full ownership of Cove Island, which later became known as Brown's Island. In 1794, Brown acquired an additional 800 acres from Benjamin Johnston, which made him one of the largest landowners in Holliday's Cove.

The rugged war veteran soon became active in the defense of the Cove, as the threat of Indian attacks still existed. As noted in *History of Weirton, West Virginia* by David Javersak, in the winter of 1792, Brown chaired a citizens committee "for the defense of the border." A letter to the lieutenant of Washington County stated, "They resolved not to serve on militia duty in any other part of the country but where they reside." They asked for militia, blockhouses, and general assistance to "do everything for us our dangerous situation requires." The matter was resolved in a final campaign against Indian tribes of Ohio, when General "Mad Anthony" Wayne led several thousand troops to battle. "His army was the largest ever to descend the Ohio, passing Holliday's Cove in late April or early May in 1793." Brown also served as a local magistrate.

The colonel owned a number of slaves, including, a mulatto slave woman named Nell, who served as Honor Brown's personal maid; Toby a trusted servant; and several other field hands. When Hugh Brown arrived on the island, the two brothers worked alongside the field slaves to clear the land and cultivate the rich, fertile soil. Richard built his farmhouse cabin and shelter for his slaves near the south end of the island, overlooking lush fields of wheat and corn.

Abundant crops of all varieties flourished. In addition to his success in farming, Brown also developed a keen sense for business. Reuben Gold Thwaites wrote in his *Journal* after visiting the colonel and his wife Honor, "The slaves, cattle, officers of everything indicated the greatest of abundance of the produce of this plentiful country. Though he does not keep a tavern, he knows how to charge as if he did, we having to pay him a half dollar for our plain supper, plainer bed and two quarts of milk we took with us the next morning, which was very high in a country where cash is very scarce and everything else very abundant."

As Brown continued to prosper from his farming and other business ventures, he constructed a grist mill on the Ohio side. This was believed to have been the first dam built on the Ohio River. He also built a home on the mainland in the cove for his wife Honor, while he continued to live in his farmhouse cabin on the island. Their three children—Richard Jr., Rachel, and Margaret---were grown when the house was built. Richard, Jr., was a county surveyor who also held the offices of sheriff and justice of the peace. He served in the militia for seven years and he achieved the rank of colonel.

Hugh and Ruth Brown built their cabin near the river bank just across from Brown's Island on the Virginia side. As described in *Recollections of an Itinerate Life* by George Brown (their youngest son), George had spent his playful boyhood on the island "amid the beauty and grandeur of that romantic place" where he often met with friends. They would run freely through the open fields, explore the woodlands, and swim and fish from the banks of the river. George wrote in his book, "I could swim the Ohio River equal to any Indian before I was eight years of age." Throughout his youth, George—by his own admission--was noted for his mischievous and sometimes reckless ways.

In 1811, the Brown family suffered two devastating losses. On February 8, Col. Richard Brown died at the age of 71. He was described by his nephew George as "a real Western pioneer; a man of great physical and mental energy, universally accepted for his usefulness as a citizen, and for his genuine benevolence of heart."

His place of burial is listed as St. John Cemetery, Colliers, West Virginia, Brooke County.

That same year on July 11, Hugh Brown died in an accident on the Ohio River. Hugh and his family had left the tranquil beauty of Brown's Island in 1800. They moved from their small cabin near the river bank to a place called Cedar-Lick Run in Jefferson County, Ohio. George Brown recounts in his book the circumstances of his father's death. "Word came by swift messenger that my aunt Honor, widow of my uncle Richard, was sick and supposed to be near death. Immediately my father and I went to see her — he on horseback and I on foot. The distance was fifteen miles . . . when we came to the river it was very low, and we both crossed on the same horse. The next morning, my father, on his return homeward, was seen, by myself and others, to cross from the Virginia shore to the island in safety. But, on the Ohio side of the island, instead of inclining a little upstream, to the out-coming place, he kept too straight over and got in very deep water, where he and his horse were both drowned." His body was recovered three days later on the Ohio side, about one mile and a half above Steubenville — so swollen that he was not recognizable. A sea shell found in his pocket (common to Brown's Island) led to the identification of his body. He is buried in the Presbyterian Cemetery in Steubenville, Ohio.

Hugh would have been proud of his youngest son George, a boy who had been known for his reckless ways. George had put aside the mistakes of his youth and, in later years, rose to prominence as a minister in the Methodist Church. In 1821, in the seventh year of his ministry, George married Eliza Jackson of Washington, Pennsylvania.

The bereaved family of Richard Brown took comfort from the generous provisions in his will. (*History of Hancock County*,

Virginia and West Virginia, by Jack Welch). He desired that his wife Honor "be rendered as comfortable the remainder of her days as possible." As a result, she was able to maintain her house in the Cove with the help of her servant Nell, who would be set free at Honor's death. Toby, their trusted servant, would be set free at his master's death. The remainder of the slaves and other possessions would be sold at auction. Honor would also receive rent from the island and 1/3 the value of the estate. The island was not to be sold until all debts were paid.

To the colonel's grandson Richard, son of Richard, Jr., who lived with him, he gave 100 acres of land "lying on the waters of Sandy Creek—Tuscarawas County, state of Ohio" and two of his prized colts.

His son Richard, Jr., inherited a large tract of land in Somerset County, Pennsylvania, and 1/3 the value of the sale of Brown's Island. Richard married Barbara Nessley in 1798. They lived in Holliday's Cove for a time and eventually settled further north near Tomlinson Run. He died in 1849.

Brown's two daughters, Rachel and Margaret, each inherited 1/3 the value of the estate and a "part of the rent of the farm I now live on with the island." Rachel had married James Wells. Her younger sister Margaret became Mrs. Thomas Madden. Both were married prior to their journey west, and little is known as to where they settled. Rachel died November 14, 1815, and was buried in Greenfield Township, Fairfield County, Ohio. Margaret had migrated further west and passed away in 1838 in St. Genevive, Missouri.

Colonel Richard Brown earned his place in history as the first settler to carve out a homestead on Brown's Island in the dense forest of an untamed wilderness. He is also recognized as one of the co-founders of Holliday's Cove, along with John Holliday, Harmon Greathouse, and James Campbell.

The courage shown by the Brown family on their long perilous journey west to Holliday's Cove, Virginia marked the beginning of a very fascinating and storied island.

THE INCREDIBLE JOURNEY OF SARAH KINNEY LEWIS

Author's note: *The following narrative of Sarah Kinney Lewis is true. It is based on legal papers and other materials held in the archives of the Eva Brook Donly Museum in Simcoe, Ontario, Canada, in a folder labeled Tynsdale Law Firm, filed under "Blacks of Norfolk County". Sarah was the inspiration for the historical novel,* Sarah's Journey, *by Canadian author David Beasley.* —Mary Zwierzchowski

Slavery came to Brown's Island with the arrival of Colonel Richard Brown. He arrived in Holliday Cove, Virginia around 1786 with his wife, two children, and an entourage of slaves. Among them was a mulatto woman named Molly Kinney.

In 1790, Molly gave birth on Brown's Island to a girl named Sarah. Sarah's father was Colonel Richard Brown, slave master and owner of the island named for him. Molly died in childbirth leaving Sarah, whose slave name was Sal, to be raised by house servants. Sarah knew by the age of six that her happy childhood had passed away. Soon she would be trained in the ways of slavery.

Sarah grew up amid the pleasant surroundings of Brown's Island, working in the fields and sharing in household duties. She belonged to a peculiar class of beauty known as octoroons—one eighth black. The olive tint of her complexion, long black wavy hair, and large bright eyes made her stand out among the darker slaves. Despite the difference, she received no special treatment from Richard Brown, her father of Dutch ancestry.

Sarah Kinney was a good-looking young woman who soon caught the eye of a newcomer to the Cove, a Negro named Henry Lewis, who introduced himself to her as a free man. With permission from Colonel Brown, Sarah and Henry eventually married. Sarah hoped that her marriage to Henry—a free man—would bring her one step closer to gaining her freedom. If only Henry could save enough money, she thought, perhaps then he could buy her way out of slavery.

Henry and Sarah lived and worked on the island less than 100 yards from freedom on the Ohio shore, where slavery was outlawed. Sarah carried out her duties as a slave while Henry worked at odd jobs wherever he could find them. They had two children, Henry and Mary. Their greatest contentment came from being together as a family. But as time passed, their life in Holliday's Cove began to change.

Henry, who had presented himself as a free man, was discovered to be a runaway slave. Chased down by bounty hunters, he was soon captured and taken back to his owner in Kentucky. Sarah was left to raise the children on her own. Her dream of being free had been taken from her.

Tragedy struck again on a cold night in February, 1811, when at the age of 71 Colonel Richard Brown passed away. If there was no provision for Sarah in Brown's will, she would be in danger of being sold or—even worse—separated from her children. The Colonel had provided generously for his wife Honor and their three children—Richard, Rachael, and Margaret. Honor Brown's personal maid Nell would be set free, as well as their servant Toby.

Secrets in the Mist

But the will made no mention of the name Sarah or Sal. Once again, her chance to be free had slipped away. Sal would be sold to the highest bidder along with the remaining slaves.

Sarah and her two children were purchased by a neighboring farmer, James Campble, a man noted for his ill temper and frequent bouts of drunkenness. His mistreatment of Sarah made her yearn for the more pleasant days spent on Brown's Island with Henry and the children. Weary of his abuse, Sarah took a bold step toward gaining her freedom legally.

In 1818, a lawsuit was filed in Brooke County Court on behalf of Sarah and others *(Sal and other black persons vs. James Campble)*, charging Campble with "assault and battery and false imprisonment." Court records revealed that when Richard Brown brought his slaves from Maryland to Holliday's Cove, he had not properly registered them within the allotted time. Sarah's mother, Molly Kinney, had died and was never registered. The lawsuit claimed that Sarah, therefore, was not legally a slave and that she and her children should be set free. The twelve white jurors assigned to the trial—also slaveholders—failed to return a verdict, and the case was dismissed.

Campble became enraged by the legal action Sarah had taken against him. In retaliation, he sold Sarah and her children to a slave-trader. They were taken from the Campble farm and sent ten miles south to Wellsburg, where they were placed in a holding pen near the town square. They would be kept there until the day of auction.

Sarah faced the dreaded fear of being sold to a distant plantation in the Deep South. She would rather risk death than be subjected to the extreme cruelty of a southern slaver.

With the help of friends and others who were sympathetic to her cause, Sarah planned her escape. On a very dark night in early spring, Sarah slipped the bonds of her captors and with her children at her side, made her way north to a waiting boat. They huddled together against the night chill as they were taken across the river to the Ohio shore near Steubenville, Ohio, where Sarah would begin her incredible journey to freedom.

With few provisions, they set out together on the long perilous trail northward through the Ohio wilderness, where they endured many hardships. They joined other fugitive slaves to ward off the constant threat of local sheriffs, slave catchers, or civilian lynch mobs and were often hungry and in need of rest. Their only comfort came from the occasional safe houses along the way, where they would be provided with a hiding place, food, and — at times — transportation to help them get further north on their dangerous road to freedom. For those who endured the long grueling journey with its many hardships, Canada was the Promised Land.

After many weeks of trekking through the harsh wilderness, Sarah and her children arrived in Canada. They settled in Simcoe, Ontario, where Sarah met a young Scot entrepreneur named Duncan Campbell, who hired her as his housekeeper. Duncan took in Sarah and her children and treated them kindly. It was Sarah's first real taste of freedom.

In 1824, while living in Duncan's house, Sarah gave birth to a son, John Lewis. Although no supporting documents could be found, there exists a strong belief that Duncan Campbell was John's father. John grew up in the Campbell household and was properly educated. His fair complexion and lack of Negro traits prompted him to make a life-altering decision. He planned to travel to New York City to seek his fortune and, in the process, pass himself off as white. But it would come at a price.

In order to hide his background, John had to reject his Brown's Island heritage and deny that Sarah was his mother. Through the years, Sarah had very little direct contact with him and would look forward to his occasional letters.

In mid-life, with her children grown, Sarah left the Campbell house and set out on her own. She was twelve years older than the prospering young Scotsman and realized early on that he would eventually choose a wife from the upper level of society. They parted on good terms and met often to discuss John's welfare. Sarah moved to a small cottage across from a deer park owned by Duncan. She relied on her domestic skills to support herself and for the very first time felt truly independent.

Sarah was content in knowing that her children were doing well. Her daughter, who lived near her, had become a talented dressmaker. John had found great success in the financial markets of New York City and became a millionaire.

Duncan Campbell, with his acumen for business, had risen to lofty heights in the world of finance and was highly regarded in Simcoe as one of the town's wealthiest and most influential citizens. He married the daughter of a naval captain and built a large pretentious-looking house of notable architectural significance. It served as Campbell's home for over forty years and was often the setting for gatherings of important and famous people. It was designated a National Historic Site for its architectural features and serves today as the Norfolk Arts Centre. Duncan Campbell is regarded as one of the founding pioneers of Simcoe.

In her later years, Sarah once again fell on hard times. She developed dementia. While on a trip to see her grandchildren, she became confused and mistakenly took the wrong train north to Barrie on Lake Simcoe, a strange town where no one knew her.

She had spent what little money she had with her and was seen wandering the streets of Barrie for several weeks—cold, hungry and ragged. A concerned citizen reported her plight to authorities. They arrested Sarah for vagrancy and placed her in the Barrie Jail. Unable to explain where she lived, she would remain there until her memory was restored or someone claimed her.

Sarah's two older children, Henry and Mary, did not have enough money or political clout to arouse public interest in the disappearance of their mother. Duncan and John, despite their wealth and power, were reluctant to use their influence to find Sarah for fear of unraveling the same long-held secret they both harbored—their very intimate and irrevocable ties to Sarah, a former slave.

Sarah languished in Barrie prison through spring and summer. John arrived too late to be of any help. Sarah had died. Since no one came to claim her, she was buried without ceremony in the Wesleyan burial ground on the hill behind the prison.

John purchased a proper tombstone for his mother, neatly inscribed—"SACRED TO THE MEMORY OF SARAH LEWIS, NATIVE OF U.S.A., WHO DEPARTED THIS LIFE AUGUST 19, 1862, AGED 72 YEARS."

As noted in the final chapter of *Sarah's Journey* by David Beasley, "Sarah's grave, despite John Lewis's care to have her remembered with a fitting tombstone, disappeared when the Wesleyan burial ground in Barrie gave way to development."

The untimely death of John Lewis in 1874, at the age of fifty, and subsequent legal papers filed in the settlement of his estate, led to the discovery of Sarah and her inspiring story.

From Brown's Island, Virginia, to Simcoe, Canada, Sarah Kinney Lewis had lived her life in the shadows of greatness of those she had dutifully served. The true greatness, however, would be found within Sarah, herself, for her remarkable display of courage and resourcefulness on her long, arduous, most incredible journey to freedom.

Above, Reverend George Brown. From "Recollections from an Itinerant Life." Below, Emanuel Hooker

Chapter Seventeen

THE HOOKER FAMILY

The Hooker family reflected the large family sizes showing up in early US censuses. In 1790, close to thirty-six percent of families numbered more than seven persons in a household. In 1850 family sizes with seven to nine children were normal. Between 1860 and 1920, family size peaked and then the number of children began to decrease. Parents considered children an economic asset. Having a higher number of heirs ensured them of family members to care for them in their old age. In the early 1800s, an average of eighty-two percent of the population farmed the land as the Hookers did.

Attitudes in Hooker's time towards women were that they should be happy in their role as housewives and find their fulfillment there. Men were to "go out in the world."

The Hooker family's account begins with Thomas, who lived ten miles from Baltimore near Ricetown, Maryland. His son Richard was born on September 24, 1701. He made his living by farming and planting tobacco. In his account book and family record, he wrote a summary of his philosophy: "Grace, wisdom, and understanding is a fine thing."[sic]

Mr. Richard Hooker married Martha, and they had thirteen children. Unfortunately, only three children left records, and those three were Eurath, Richard, and Samuel. The group moved to Greenfield township in Fairfield County, Ohio, in 1810. Not too much is known about Eurath, the oldest of the three, born on December 4, 1736. She never married.

Richard, born October 20, 1745, also remained unmarried. He purchased large tracts of land and served on the Board of Directors of the First Lancaster Bank in Lancaster, Ohio. He entered politics, first as a representative for four terms and then as a senator for two terms in the legislature of Ohio. Richard gave farms to the children of his brother Samuel.

Samuel, born November 16, 1757, married Rachel Belt of Maryland. He purchased 665 acres of land west of Hooker Station, Ohio. He and his wife had six children. Their family gained prominence in Greenfield Township, close to Lancaster. His son Richard, born February 17, 1799, married Phoebe Tallman.

The Tallman family lived on a farm in Amanda Township. Their family included two daughters who each married two different men named Richard Hooker. In 1806 Nancy Tallman (Phoebe's sister) married a Richard Hooker related to Samuel and Richard, sons of Thomas Hooker from Maryland. Nancy's husband was known as "Turkey Run Hooker," or "Dick" to differentiate him from the other Richard Hooker. Richard "Turkey Run Hooker," born in Maryland in November 1776, purchased Brown's Island on May 23, 1828.

Before moving to Brown's Island, Richard bought sections of land on Turkey Run, Ohio in 1811. He put a grist mill on that part of the land. He gave an acre of ground for a graveyard and a schoolyard. The land also served to hold a Baptist church. The land proved fertile and offered pleasing vistas.

When he moved to Brooke County (now Hancock) in West

Virginia, he bought land on the mainland and Brown's Island. He took a prominent place in the community of Holliday's Cove and the surrounding area. He and his wife Nancy had twelve children: Richard, Emanuel (died at 3 years), Phoebe, Minerva, George, Emanuel (same name as their first child), Elizabeth, Tallman, Nancy, Samantha (died at 18 months), Mary Jane, and John Randolph. Nancy married Darwin Stanton, whose brother Edwin Stanton rose to a position as Abraham Lincoln's Secretary of War.

When Richard Hooker, the father, died, he arranged for Emmanuel to have Brown's Island and Tallman to receive the property in Holliday's Cove. His oldest son Richard had property in the Fairfield area but sold the property to purchase land in Steubenville, Ohio.

Emanuel lived until 49 but packed a lot of adventure into his life. He married three times and had seven children. He served in two wars and joined the wanderlust movement that beckoned him west to California. Emanuel married twice while he lived in Holliday's Cove. Marriage records from Jefferson County show that Emanuel married first Mary Jane Doyle in 1838, who died young. Her grave rests in the Union Cemetery of Steubenville with her original Doyle family.

His second union in 1842 was to Mary Jane Bishop, who lived in Ohio. They married in Steubenville, Ohio. In 1846, Emmanuel and his wife Mary Jane sold Brown's Island to Lorenzo and Sumner Jewett. Emmanuel then served in the Mexican War from 1846 until 1848; according to California, Pioneer Migration Index compiled 1906-1935. He sailed to Matamoros City, Mexico. At 29, he enlisted in the 3rd regiment of the Ohio Volunteer Infantry and was appointed to a sergeant's position. The Mexican American War revolved around border disputes relating to Texas. His regiment was part of Zachary Taylor's Army of the Rio Grande. The war ended with America gaining property from Texas to California as part of its concept of manifest destiny. Emanuel returned to Ohio with the title of second lieutenant. He then got caught up in Gold Rush fever heading a company sending wagons to California. In the 1850 Census, Emanuel is listed as head of household in Richland, Madison, Ohio. By this time, his mother Nancy lived with him as well as Mary Jane and six children. He then took his family to California, and one of his children was born en route. His wife died in 1856, and he returned to Ohio.

Emmanuel also served during the Civil War, in the 1st Ohio Volunteer Infantry. He quickly moved up the ranks, as first lieutenant, captain and then a major. He was wounded badly in the Battle of Shiloh, a bitter battle in Tennessee in April of 1862. After coming home to recover, he rejoined his unit, finally mustering out in August 1864. He returned and served in the 179th Ohio Volunteer Infantry. Then he married his third wife and he had one more child. Finally, he died in Lancaster, Ohio. In his obituary, it states he died in Lancaster on August 11 at the age of 49. The last two sentences of his obituary read, "As a citizen, he was honorable. As a soldier, he was brave to a fault, and in his death, our city has lost a useful, active citizen, and the country a noble defender."

Tallman Hooker stayed in Holliday's Cove, living on the property he inherited, and he and his wife Sarah had three children. He built a brick home across from Brown's Island where Hugh and Ruth Brown had formerly lived in a cabin. Their son George visited his uncle Colonel Richard Brown on Brown's Island, where he had a merry time. Tallman Hooker took over his father's home, and John Crawford had purchased land in North Weirton. Crawford's homestead was across from what became the Bank of Weirton and is now a church. In the *History of Holliday's Cove* by Mary Shakley Ferguson wrote; "These two homes standing there among the wide green fields were equal to southern mansions."

The Hooker Family

In a Western Pennsylvania account on the Crawfords, they speak of the properties of these men as extending to the Ohio River. The author mentions the Crawford property as being "just south of the ferry to Brown's Island which was operated from land owned by the Hooker family."

Tallman's son Richard "Dick" Hooker grew tired of farming the land, and in Mary's account, "he built the machine shop in upper Cove where farmers could buy and get mending done on their farm machinery...Richard kept a large supply of nails and building tools for this growing community."

Mary Ferguson described Dick's character as rough and untidy, but he was a man of means. He had his eye on Levinia Hindman, a pretty, young woman who passed by his machine shop quite a bit in her travels. She, however, was said to be in love with a poor lawyer who had little. Levinia's parents urged her to marry Dick Hooker so that she could lead a comfortable life. However, as the story went, this money did not buy her happiness. Dick and Levinia had a daughter Iris who attended the Female Seminary in Steubenville. Iris played the organ at the Christian Church and gave music lessons, which allowed her to view ideas for a home. She had big round ice blue eyes. She stayed single and eventually moved into a house that stood on the corner of Main Street and Marland Heights Road, close to where United Bank is now situated. After looking at others' furniture, Iris never did buy much for her house, and it was said she had to uncover a chair for guests when they came to her house.

Iris died in 1949 at age 77. Her obituary in the *Weirton Daily Times* listed that she was born in Holliday's Cove at the Hindman farm on August 30, 1872. She died at a friend's home on West Street, where she had lived for the last nine years of her life as her health failed. The paper noted Iris Hooker's service as a former organist at the Christian Church. Even though her great-grandparents had raised a large family, she had no known survivors in the area. Her grave is in Union Cemetery in Steubenville, Ohio.

Other brothers of Tallman who had been in the area moved from the area along with their families. It appears that Tallman married again, although there are no records for either of his marriages. In the 1880 census of Hancock County, he is listed as head of his household with Margaret listed as his wife, Margaret Teasdale as a servant, and Margaret Bilderback as a niece. Tallman Hooker died August 7, 1898 at the age of 77.Early members of the Hooker family had graves in the Three Springs Cemetery on Three Springs Drive Road in Weirton, West Virginia. A stone commemorating Richard Hooker, the original Hooker owning the Brown's Island property, lies in the cemetery. Tallman's sister Phebe also rests in the cemetery. She had married a Claypool, and that is her name on the stone. Tallman and his first wife Sarah are buried together, and Margaret Hooker is also interred in the cemetery. She would have most likely been Tallman's second wife. Richard Hooker, son of Tallman, is buried with his wife Anna (short for Levinia), originally Hindman. By coming to the area, the Hooker family purchased the island and a portion of the mainland that would hold the original Weirton Steel blast furnace.

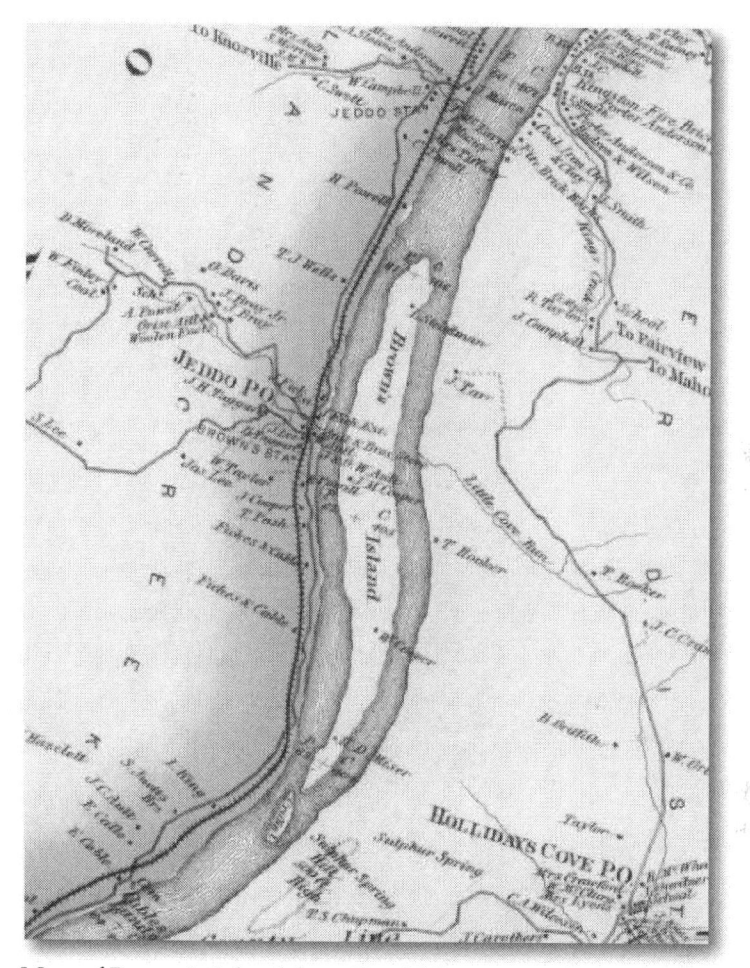

Map of Brown's Island from David Rumsey Collection 1877. Map shows residences of Lyman Stedman to the north, and James Cooper in the middle. Wellington Cooper's residence is in lower half of island and the Miser property is in the south. The Hooker properties became the site of the mainland Weirton Steel properties where the original coke plant set.

Chapter Eighteen

JOINED BY A MARRIAGE: THE JEWETTS AND THE STEDMANS

In the 1800s, changes in water and land transportation made traveling in the area easier. Bob Petras from Toronto, Ohio, talks about the changes to the river and dams around the Browns Island area. The *New Orleans* was the first steamboat to travel down the Ohio River from around Pittsburgh, Pennsylvania in 1811. After that, steamboats proliferated and numbered over 650, making way for industrial growth.

Sand and gravel bars stalled traffic as in the Lewis and Clark expedition. The summer heat caused water levels to sink. In the winter, cold created ice which jammed and would often melt and cause flooding in January thaws. Bob says, "Boating companies pressured the federal government to improve navigation conditions, and thus, in 1824, Congress authorized the U.S. Army Corps of Engineers to remove snags and other obstructions from the Ohio River. At the same time, they constructed dikes and wing dams to concentrate flow into the main channel."

In 1836 the Corps constructed dams at Brown's Island. Unfortunately, the channel weaved along the Ohio side and the "dike," as the locals called the first dam built, caused this higher water to flow to the Virginia side. "The Corps added a crescent-shaped wing dam less than a half-mile downstream on the Virginia shore to deflect flowback into the channel."

The boats traversing the Ohio River in the 1800s consisted of sternwheelers and paddleboats. "A paddleboat or paddle wheeler is a ship or boat propelled by one or more paddle wheels driven by an engine. According to the Ohio Sternwheeler Festival website, boats with paddles on their sides are also called sidewheelers, while those with a single wheel on the stern are known as sternwheelers." To get around from Brown's Island to the shores of Ohio and West Virginia, the families used skiffs (small boats with flat bottoms and pointed fronts) and rowboats. The families on the island at this time witnessed a parade of watercraft on the busy Ohio River.

The Jewett family bought the land on Brown's Island from the Hookers. The Jewetts had two famous people in their family: Henri de Juatt served as a Knight in the First Crusade from 1096-99, and Deacon Maximilian Jewett founded Rowley, Massachusetts. *The History and Genealogy Jewetts of America* shows Mark Jewett as being born near Hopkinton, New Hampshire, June 15, 1762. "He married, about 1785-86, Patience Varney." She was born on August 8, 1764. Like the Hooker family in the last chapter, they produced a large family. They had ten children who were born in New Hampshire. Like many of this period, Mark Jewett made his living from the land as a farmer and stock raiser. He moved to Ohio, and he and his wife both died near Steubenville, Ohio. Patience died in 1829, and her husband Mark died in 1849 at the home of his son Sumner.

Three of Mark's sons owned property on Brown's Island. On

May 15, 1846, Lorenzo and Sumner Jewett purchased Brown's Island from Emanuel Hooker and his second wife, Mary Jane. Lorenzo and Sumner were close in age, Sumner being born on April 26, 1802 and Lorenzo two years later on June 29, 1804.

Lewis, older brother to Sumner and Lorenzo and born in 1797, purchased the north half of the land in 1857. Lewis became prosperous from farming the land in Meigs County, Ohio. He married Susan Henry near Toronto, Ohio, and they had two daughters, Patience and Emily. Patience married William Knapp in Pittsburgh, Pennsylvania and moved to Ravenna, Ohio.

Relatives of the Jewetts stayed in the Toronto area. Jeff Jewett, who grew up in Toronto, said, "My grandmother told me not to ever go over to the island." Jeff's great-great-grandfather was Sumner Jewett, who would have been Emily and Patience's uncle. Jeff's brothers and sister have all moved from the area, like many "boomers" in the Ohio Valley.

Emily Jewett married Lyman Stedman in 1850, and they raised five children. Lyman Stedman provided the most documentation about what it was like to live on Brown's Island. He kept diaries, including details of sales from his farm and daily events on the island. Lyman came from Chester, Ohio and purchased the land from William and Patience Knapp, brother-in-law, and sister of his wife.

Lyman's grandfather Levi Stedman lived in Tunbridge, Vermont, and around 1800 he became entranced with moving west to Athens, Ohio, where he could obtain cheap land. After taking a scouting trip to the area, he returned home to plan a permanent move to Ohio. Although a group of husbands hung on to their dream of going westward, the wives dreaded moving to unknown lands and leaving their relatives.

Correspondences went back and forth to those who had already moved in 1802 and 1803. After a rough spring in Vermont, Levi and his wife Dorothy (Doly) put their names on a growing list of those wishing to travel westward. Doly's sister Lucy and her husband Elezear Kingsbury joined the group. They had to adapt to the birth of babies, so they deferred their plans until 1804. All had to leave precious items to fit all the necessities and children in the wagons. Finally, in mid-June they arrived in the town of Marietta, Ohio, and in October the men had built the first cabin in Meigs County, Ohio.

Levi and Doly named their first son Lyman (Sr.). He grew up to have a son, also called Lyman. After Lyman Jr.'s episode of "consumption," his doctors recommended that he work outside instead of inside. Unfortunately, this advice kept him from pursuing a career as a lawyer.

He maintained his interest in politics, eventually serving in the West Virginia House of Delegates in 1877. He was originally a Democrat until the fall of Ft. Sumpter, then he switched to Republican. He served as Legislator for West Virginia, Farmer, Merchant; JP, and Township Clerk in Meigs Co. In the book *Smokestacks in the Hills*, author Lou Martin begins with a chapter focusing on Hancock County to represent the rural roots of West Virginia. Among other residents of the county, he writes about Lyman Stedman. Lyman reported the hard work of farming with its cycles of planting according to the seasons. In the fall of 1880, he mentions their harvesting and husking of corn, picking apples, threshing wheat, plowing, and mowing, butchering a calf, and selling livestock.

In the winter of 1880-81, his son Sedgwick attended school, while his older son Audubon helped Lyman. Together, Lyman and Audubon "butchered hogs, made sausage, hauled coal up to the house, fed the cattle, and made skiff oars out of the red elm planks." Spring and the month of April brought the tapping of maple trees and the planting of spring crops. In May they sorted apples and packed them to sell downriver. With the weather warming in the summer, they hoed land for corn and potatoes, made new fence posts, and washed and sheared sheep. They were at the mercy of the river where their island sat so that flooding would affect their crops and kept them busy dealing with its floods or dry spells."

In addition to writing about the daily events, Lyman kept up his interest in politics. In October of 1880, he wrote about selling a calf to G. W. Ault for $8. Then he continued in his abbreviated form, "A great Republican demonstration in Steubenville. The town full of folks. Listened to a splendid speech from Col. Gibson of Seneca, Co., O." Three days later he started his day with apple picking, and then, "went to election in express with Aud (his son Audubon) at Osborne's mill on Kings Creek, voted Rep. Ticket as posted on front cover.

On November 2, Lyman commented on the presidential election. "The great day of the Republicans candidate, James A. Garfield president...Republican candidates elected by decided majority."

(Note: Garfield was sworn in as president in March 1881, but an assassin shot him after six months. He died after that so that Chester Arthur would assume the presidential spot.)

Drawing of the Lyman Stedman Residence on Brown's Island. From the David Rumsey Collection, 1877.

Lyman also wrote about his family, noting his children's birthdays and seemed to understand the young people needed their fun. "An oyster supper at Audie's in hon. [honor] of his birthday. Some 30 young folk present and staid [sic] up all night on [account] of ice in river."

He made notes of visits to the other families of the island. "All went down to Miser's on the sled and spent the evening. Well [Wellington] Cooper and family went along."

In 1884 Lyman called the flood in February "The Great Flood of 1884." He wrote, "O the destruction of property and suffering in the whole Ohio Valley is wholly unprecedented in the history of the country." On February 6 the river rose all day at the rate of 10 inches an hour. He and his family kept busy trying to protect their belongings. The water crept up to their dooryard fence, and they began removing food from the basement. They tore up the carpet in the parlor bedroom and started moving things upstairs. His son provided hourly reports on the number of inches pouring down until the river finally reached 47 feet, 3 feet higher than a flood in 1832. On February 7 Stedman wrote, "5 PM the water began to recede when within 2 feet of our 1st floor."

He spent three months cleaning up the debris on his property and repairing the damages. Again, he remarked on the severity of this flood, "Congress has appropriated 300,000$ Ohio 200,000$ other municipal corporations, and private individuals are pouring in contributions by the thousands for the flood sufferers — No parallel to this flood has ever occurred since the Ohio Valley was a howling wilderness."

Lyman's wife Emily (previously a Jewett) and her two daughters Blanche and Mabel worked long and hard days on Brown's Island. At the crack of dawn, they milked the cows and hauled water. They started the fire for cooking and made bread daily. They butchered the animals for food and had to pluck the chickens. Women tended to items close to the house, so they also took care of a garden patch, fed the hogs and chicken, took care of geese, and turned milk into butter. In 1880 the family produced three hundred pounds of butter.

As if the above tasks weren't enough, they made candles and soap for the household. They "spent nights beside the fireplace making thread, cloth, and clothing. They made other items out of fabric including curtains, bedsheets, pillows, pillowcases, and mattresses which they filled with the down they plucked from geese the family had eaten that winter."

The women also helped with fieldwork when all hands were needed, such as harvest time. The family's endeavors in the field provided sustenance for the family with surplus to sell. The family unit worked efficiently and purposefully. The Stedman family represented the work of the rural life of the families on both sides of the river. The Stedmans visited with neighbors and participated in group efforts with projects, such as threshing and harvesting, building barns and houses, and assisting during illnesses. "Farm families like those of northern West Virginia identified strongly with their local communities, an identity reinforced by collective activities, kinship, ties to the land, community events and a sense of belonging."

Blanche Stedman reflected on her attachment to the land and her family when she wrote about her marriage on April 14, 1871 when she was barely nineteen. In her diary she wrote she had a happy, carefree childhood "knew only constant tender sympathy" from her father, who was always a source of help for any problem" and she wished she were "as sweet and beautiful" as her mother.

Before marrying Dr. John Riley Keyes, a Methodist-Episcopal minister, she graduated from Scio College, a seminary in Ohio where she was president of her class. On her wedding day, she remembered the weather was pleasantly warm, "It was a summer day; the apple trees were in full bloom, and the grass was green."

Blanche had five children, and she moved with her husband, who transferred churches frequently. After her husband died in 1911, she struggled to keep the house they had bought in Cambridge, Ohio a year earlier. Her husband wanted her to hold onto it so that their children could visit their original home. She supplemented her income by taking in boarders. She cut her grass into her eighties. She felt the government was at fault for not adequately funding the widows from the Civil War, in which her husband had served. Blanche lived until 85, having been alive during the Civil War, and witnessed the Franklin Delano Roosevelt years.

Lyman's son Chester would gain prominence as a doctor. He graduated from Steubenville High School in 1895. He then pursued a medical degree at Baltimore Medical College, working as a resident at St. Joseph's Hospital in Baltimore and assisting in pathology and bacteriology at the college. Next, he graduated from Army Medical School in Washington, DC. He received more graduate studies in bacteriology, physiologic chemistry, and nutrition at Sheffield Scientific School of Yale University, during 1909-1910.

He invented a section lifter and slideholder for use in pathologic laboratories in 1903. He served in the U.S. Army Medical Corps as a first lieutenant and captain traveling to various posts in the United States and Alaska and had a private practice in Oregon in 1910 and 1911.

Chester passed away at only 38 in July 1916 at Fort Bayard, New Mexico. His father passed away later the same year at age 88 in November on Brown's Island

Chapter Nineteen

THE ISLAND DIVIDES
COOPER, MISER AND MAGINNIS FAMILIES

In 1860 James Cooper bought the south half of the island. Two years later, he sold the half of his property on the island to his son Wellington Cooper and Henry D. Miser for $6500. In 1886 Wellington Cooper and his wife sold Henry D. Miser his half of the south half of Brown's Island for $100. Henry Miser employed Harry Maginnis as a servant in his house. Maginnis and his wife Susan Cooper became owners of the Miser properties in 1913 when Wellington's daughter Mary and her husband Samuel Taylor sold the property to the McGinnises for a dollar.

James Cooper was the son of Ephraim Cooper, who was believed to have been born close to Baltimore, Maryland. He married Matilda Henry, and they had eight children.

Wellington Cooper, son of James, was born in February 1831 in Ohio. He married Mercy Bray, and they had two daughters, Mary and Susan. 49 showed up in the U.S. Civil War Draft Registration Records, 1863-1865. He became a brother-in-law to Henry Miser when Henry married Mercy's sister Rachel. Census records list Wellington in the censuses of West Virginia in 1870 and 1880. By 1900 he and his wife moved to Toronto in Jefferson County, Ohio.

His wife passed away in 1909, and three years later, Wellington died of heart problems. In his obituary, he is noted as a member of the Presbyterian Church in Toronto. The listing also describes his character traits of honesty, integrity, kindness, and consideration. He impressed the community, and he was a "delightful companion to the young as well as the elderly, and his memory will live in the hearts of relatives and friends as an exemplary Christian gentleman."

In 1880 his daughter Mary married a prominent attorney in Toronto, Ohio named Samuel B. Taylor. Samuel's grandfather Richard moved to America from Ireland around 1770 and farmed in Washington County, Pennsylvania. Samuel, born in Jefferson County, finished his college education in Hopedale and Richdale and taught for thirteen years. He then became a merchant in Mooretown for three years. Samuel also studied law while he served as the mayor of Toronto for two terms. Next, he opened a law office in Toronto. His interest in politics and the Republican Party led him to run for the state legislature. He was a member from 1892-1896. The Taylors had two children, Ella and Jay. Their son unfortunately passed away in infancy.

Henry Miser's parents were David and Mary Powell, originally from Lancaster, Pennsylvania, became pioneer residents of Jefferson County, Ohio. Henry was born in Annapolis, Ohio, in 1828.

Henry married Rachel Bray in Steubenville in April of 1854. Her sister Mercy married Wellington Cooper, who thus became his brother-in-law. Henry bought a part of the southern part of Brown's Island, and in 1862, he and his brother-in-law farmed the island for forty-five years. In 1886 Wellington and his wife sold them their land. Henry moved to Toronto. Henry had sight in only one eye for 59 years and then lost sight in his other eye 17 years later. His home on the island was hospitable, and his friends would visit him on the island. He moved to Steubenville when his health declined. In his obituary he was lauded for his good character. "During Mr. Miser's business activities in this county, he was well known in all sections, and his many friends will mourn the loss of one whom they would call their friend and who was a Christian man of excellent character. He was a member of the Hamline M.E. Church."

Henry and his wife left no children. At his death his wife Rachel, a brother, and three sisters survived him. Art Miser, a descendant of Henry's family, whose parents lived in Weirton, said the family reunions were so large that they had to rent all of Marland Heights Pool to have room for the festivities. In the 1950s, many relatives in the Cooper, Miser, and other families were still in the area. Henry died on his birthday on August 25, 1914.

He hired Harry McGinnis at age 17 to help him with the farm and wished for Harry to have his land. Harry's family had moved to the area from Pennsylvania. He married Susan, daughter of Wellington Cooper, who gave the land to them.

They had ten or eleven children (records vary). Harry McGinnis took the position of police/judge in 1917 for Holliday's Cove. He was on the payroll of Weirton Steel. Known to be a happy, sociable man, Harry operated a small ferryboat to take workers across the river. "He farmed the island at this time, according to a friend of his wife. He took on an unusual role in local history and a special place in the hearts of the mill workers. The steel mill paid them every Saturday, and since there weren't many drinking opportunities in Weirton, they headed over to Steubenville, Ohio to celebrate. It was McGinnis' job to get them across the wide Ohio River and safely home again.

According to the anecdote, the men gathered at the West

Virginia riverbank, and McGinnis ferried them across to the Ohio shore. Some got rowdy on the return trip, but the squire was a big man, and when he told them to sit down, they sat. Then he got them off on the West Virginia side and lined them up by a fence post for a count. McGinnis boasted that he never lost a man."

In the 1910 census, the records show the following people living on the island: Lyman, Mabel, and Audubon Steadman; the McGinnis family with their children; the William M. Porter family; and the Cyrus Allen family. The first three families farmed the island for their livelihood, while Cyrus Allen served as a minister. Reverend Allen's wife was Margaret, called "Maggie," the daughter of Tallman Hooker, who owned the land across from the island. Maggie's mother, Margarett, 79, held onto her husband's property even though Weirton Steel wanted the property, valuing its proximity to the river.

Cyrus Allen, born in Grove City, Pennsylvania, attended public schools and graduated from Grove City College. He did post-graduate work at Wooster College, Ohio, originally a Presbyterian College. Cyrus also graduated from the Western Theological Seminary in Washington, Pennsylvania, now merged into Pittsburgh-Xenia Seminary Campus. His first parish was the Cove Presbyterian Church, where he served for twenty years. Next, Reverend Allen ministered at the Paris Presbyterian Church. He also organized the first Union Sabbath Schools in Weirton in 1910. Hundreds mourned his death at 79 for his fifty years of service in the church.

SAMUEL BARNELL: Keeper of the Lights

In 1870 the federal government established a light system along the Ohio River, marking the channels day and night from its confluence at Pittsburgh and down the Mississippi. Brown's

The Island Divides Cooper, Miser and Maginnis Families

Island was one of those places where workers installed federal marking lights.

The first government light keeper assigned to Brown's Island was Samuel Barnell. He took charge of the lights in the island's vicinity and kept the kerosene lamps burning brightly. The lighthouse, which stood at the head of Brown's Island, gave guidance to oncoming steamboats as they made their descent down the Ohio River and through the narrow channel.

Barnell appeared in Holliday's Cove around 1870 from parts unknown. "No one knew where he had come from or why," notes historian Mary Ferguson. Questions about his "secret" past gave rise to an aura of mystery that remained with him throughout his career. His reticence to discuss his previous life led to the creation of imaginary tales. Some surmised that a disappointing love affair had caused him to seek the solitude of Brown's Island. Others in the cove believed it was his "crooked" past that forced him to find refuge among the thick forest of this very remote and peaceful place. None of these tales seemed to have any real foundation.

The mysterious lightkeeper, described as "a handsome man with a long white beard," built a small cabin among the thick hillside forest in view of passing boats. He lived there alone, doing his own cooking and household chores, and was seldom seen by anyone. His reluctance to mingle with folks in the cove caused him to be named "the hermit of Brown's Island."

He was a colorful character who became well known among riverboat pilots. "When boats passed by, they would sound their whistles. He would come out and salute and then would retire to his cabin again," according to an excerpt in the *20th Century History of Steubenville and Jefferson County.*

Despite his secluded way of life, which fostered numerous

mythical tales, Barnell remained faithful to his work as the keeper of the lights for more than 30 years. Unfortunately, he passed away in 1904 at the age of 78.

Even in death, the old lamplighter continued to stir controversy, as local historians disagree on the circumstances of his demise. Mary Ferguson, in *History of Holliday's Cove*, uses a "cloak-and-dagger" approach in describing the manner in which he died. She writes, "One dark night, with no moon to guide the river traffic, the light there at Brown's Island failed to pierce that darkness. In 30 years, Samuel Barnell has never failed to light that light at dusk and turn it out by daylight. The keeper of the light would not have failed his duty unless prevented in some unusual manner. Dave Hale, on his way to Taylor's Mill that morning, was apprehended by Cyrus Allen, and together the two men climbed the hill to Barnell's cabin. They found the aging man bound and gagged, the soles of his feet burned black. He regained consciousness enough to tell how two young men came to his door on the previous evening demanding money. He tried to tell them that he barely made enough to supply his meager needs and had no money. They beat and tortured him unmercifully, trying to make him tell where he had hidden the gold. The 'old hermit,' as he was commonly known, lived but a few days."

In the *20th Century History of Steubenville and Jefferson County*, a more direct approach is taken in an effort to rectify the misguided notions regarding Barnell's life and death. It notes that he "had at least one grown-up son who lived in the neighborhood, took the daily papers, was up on current events, and was familiar with prominent public men. He came to Steubenville whenever necessary to procure provisions or transact other business and was always cordial and hospitable to visitors. He remained in his forest home until the infirmities of age compelled him to relinquish the place and was taken away by his son, with whom he remained until his death, so there is no mystery about that part of his life."

Samuel was laid to rest in the Hooker family plot near the river bank where he had lived. His funeral was attended by boat and dockhands and others who knew him. His resting place at the north end of Weirton—just above the Cove—remained peaceful for nearly a decade until the property gave way to development.

Some caring person thought enough of the island "hermit" to have his grave moved to Three Springs Cemetery, where he was given an impressive headstone properly inscribed: BARNELL— FOR OVER 30 YEARS THE FAITHFUL LIGHTHOUSE KEEPER AT BROWN'S ISLAND.

No matter what myth or mystery surrounding the life and death of Samuel Barnell that may have been dispelled here, his legendary figure still lives in the glow of light at the head of Brown's Island as he stands in salute to passing boats.

Chapter Twenty

MERRIMENT ON THE ISLAND AND OTHER NOTABLE EVENTS

October 1811 – THE GREAT PUMPKIN FLOOD -- Brown's Island has been plagued with many destructive floods, but none as bizarre as the deluge of 1811. The flood was disastrous to Holliday's Cove, washing out grist and sawmills, clearing the land of corn stalks, corn cribs, haystacks and fences—including the abundant pumpkin crops from Brown's Island and other places upstream. The pumpkins came floating down the swollen river—thousands of them—bobbing up and down. According to *The History of Hollidays Cove,* by Mary Ferguson, it "created a lot of merriment as well as drawing crowds to the river front to see the parade. That Halloween, the greatest pumpkin bobbing on earth took place here near the Cove Valley."

July 4, 1882 –THE SCIOTI JOHN LOMAS COLLISION – A serious boat accident resulted in the loss of seventy-five young people. The Scioti steamboat picked up passengers in Wellsville and south towards Moundsville to attend a tour sponsored by the Wellsville cornet band. Their load of passengers numbered around six hundred, way over the 60-passenger limit. After spending hours in Moundsville the boat headed north. Passengers drank during the event, but Captain Thomas remained sober. As the

Scioti headed north, the John Lomas steamboat took return picnickers from Brown's Island to points south. They neared each other around Mingo. he John Lomas.

According to navigational standards, the descending boat chose his path and signaled with a long blast indicating he would take the Ohio side. The Scioti returned a double blast warning that he would also take the Ohio. The pilot of the John Lomas answered two more signals announcing he would change to the West Virginia side. Instead, he veered directly into path of the Scioti. With much confusion on board including news of a possible fire. People began jumping overboard. It took three minutes for the boat to sink, and young people lost their lives.

After the accident, the Federal Court drew up more specific procedures of signaling. One part said if either boat was confused when within 800 yards apart, short blasts would be blown and engines would idle until clarification.

New York Times, March 16, 1888 – COAL BARGES WRECKED – "The most disastrous wreck that has occurred on the Ohio River for 15 years happened near Steubenville yesterday. The towboats *Ed Roberts, Sam Clark*, and the *Eagle*, which left the city on Tuesday, collided at Brown's Island, near Steubenville, at 2 o'clock yesterday afternoon, piling barge upon barge in a tangled heap, and leaving no less than 40,000 bushels of coal scattered along the banks or buried in the bed of the stream. Brown's Island is in the middle of the river about 5 miles above Steubenville Bridge. To the left of the navigator as he descends the stream, and almost directly opposite the northern end of the island, is a sand bar. Below this again there is a small dam, intended for the purpose of heightening the water level off the southern end of the island." An eyewitness gave this account to a *Times* reporter. "The *Ed Roberts*, which was bound for Louisville, had just turned into the channel at the upper end of the island when the first barge struck the sand bar and began to sink, and when the pilot, seeing the danger, tried to hold the tow back he found that the violence of the current rendered it impossible. Bang! Went the edge of the island. Now the *Sam Clark*, which had been following the *Roberts* down at a distance of about 800 yards, unexpectedly appeared at the head of the island, and everybody saw that she was going to try to run the blockade. The channel was full. That was plain, and we couldn't understand why the *Clark* should try to go through, but she came crowding on and the first thing she struck was the *Roberts*, which she sent up dry on the island. The *Clark's* pilot just swore a little more than usual and shot ahead. He passed the dam with its covering of wreck and landed below without a hair turned, but he just lost by the operation one barge and five boats of the three barges and eight boats with which he approached the island. Two barges and three boats escaped being sunk or piled up on *Roberts's* wreck."

The collision and ensuing cleanup disrupted river traffic until June 12, 1888. William Martin, head of that operation, reported finding "twenty-one coal boats and barges stranded and scattered from the head to the foot of the island."

Steubenville Herald Star, August 17, 1894 – SUNDAY AT CAMP – "The St. Paul's choir camp at Brown's Island was brilliantly illuminated last night with strings of Chinese lanterns artistically arranged. The view from Brown's station on Ohio side was that of a fairy scene. The large streamer painted by J. K. Myers was put in position today. The fish are beginning to suffer. Mr. and Mrs. Charles Specht drove up to the camp on last evening, taking with them a freezer of ice cream and box of cake, to which it is needless to say, the boys did full justice, not forgetting a compliment of cheers for the generous donors. A picnic party went up in the afternoon consisting of Misses Lattie Presley, Maude Dunbar and Bessie Dawson and Messrs. C.C. Long and Wm. Morrison."

The paper stated that "after Sunday services in the morning, a delegation called on Samuel Burnell, the lighthouse tender, and was cordially received.

Steubenville Herald Star, July 5, 1900 – A GLORIUS FOURTH – "The heat was intense all day long and thousands of people emigrated to the coolest spots to be found among the hill to enjoy themselves at picnicking. The big picnic at Brown's Island was a decided success. The steamer *T. M. Bayne* made her first trip at 8 o'clock and continued making trips all day as fast as the boat could make the round trip; still this was not sufficient to handle the large crowd of people that congregated at the foot of Market Street ready to go to the island. Fully 2,000 people went to the river, but several hundred of these were unable to go. No accidents happened to mar the pleasure of the day. The weather in the forenoon was threatening, but notwithstanding this, the morning boats handled good trips." The gala affair was one of many island celebrations.

Steubenville Herald Star, July 5, 1901 – AN OLD-FASHIONED FOURTH – "The picnic at Brown's Island was largely attended, despite the threatening weather early in the morning and the rain later, but of course many were kept away, fearing a storm. The steamers *T.M. Bayne* and *Leroy* made hourly trips during the day, handling the crowd in an admirable manner. There was no crushing as in former years, but the people were cared for in the best possible manner.

"At the island there was a merry go round, fortune wheel, shooting gallery, lunch stand and other attractions. When the rain came in the morning, the people were given shelter in the old Miser residence, which was vacated a few days since, and which proved a safe shelter during the storm.

"During the afternoon, the sun came out brightly, drying the grass when the picnicking was resumed. Owing to wet grass, the ball game did not come off nor was dancing indulged in. A swimming match was a feature in the afternoon, James Conly winning, with Gallagher and Nolan close seconds. There were several scraps during the afternoon, but no blood was spilled."

Steubenville Herald Star July 18, 1901 – TERRIFIC EXPLOSION OF NITRO-GLYCERINE – "Shortly before eight o'clock last evening a terrific explosion shook the buildings in this city. Many people at first thought it was an earthquake, but it was soon learned that a skiff load of nitroglycerine had exploded at the head of Brown's Island."

S. F. McCoy, who was floating the skiff down the river from Shamokin, Pa, told a *Herald Star* reporter the following story. He said, "I had 240 gallons of nitro-glycerine in the skiff, and knowing the stuff would gas in hot weather, I had it in two piles and each can separated. At the head of the island I put in to the shore, tied up the skiff and started up the bank to get something to eat. When I reached the railroad track, 150 yards away, the explosion occurred and threw me off the track and into the ditch. When I gathered myself together, I did not go back to where the skiff had been tied, but struck out up the railroad and crossed the river to the Ohio side the first chance I got. I do not think the glycerine exploded from bumping against the rocks. It could not have done so because I had it fixed so nothing of that kind would set it off. There were some people shooting on the other side of the river, and I think that a rifle ball struck one of the cans. In fact, I am almost positive that is what caused the explosion." According to the report, "the explosion caused considerable damage in Toronto, many windows in stores and residence being shattered."

A reporter described the aftermath. "The explosion occurred in a barren looking place today. There is a circular hole in the ground 50 feet in diameter while rocks and slimy mud is scattered over the hillside. All the foliage is stripped from the trees on the bank and many of the limbs are torn off." It was not known if there were any injuries.

Steubenville Weekly Gazette, July 11, 1902 – DEATH INVADES MERRY PICNIC PARTY AT BROWN'S ISLAND – "In the twinkling of an eye the joyousness of a merry party of Sunday school excursionists yesterday was transformed to profound sadness. In the midst of the merry-making of the children a tragedy occurred at Brown's Island ending the life of a nine-year-old girl, Lillian Smith, daughter of W.W. Smith, a tin worker, living on First Street, Martins Ferry.

"The excursion was the Sunday school picnic given by the First Baptist church of Martins Ferry, to Brown's Island on the City of Wheeling ... About 4 o'clock the little girl was sitting on a camp stool on the lower deck of the steamboat, which was moored on the island landing. The stool was near the edge of the boat. Someone called to the child and in response she jumped up. As she did so the stool fell tripping her. The child fell headlong into the water.

"Instantly several men about the boat plunged into the water to rescue the girl, but the current drew her under the boat, and she never came to the surface. Members of the crew, at the risk of their own lives groped under the boat hull, looking for the child, but the search was in vain. The boat was moved from its position and the river dragged, but no trace of the girl's body was found."

Era of Elegance: A History of Toronto, Ohio 1900-1914 by Walter M. Kestner

--Skating Accident--" Skating was popular on the Clark property south of the whiteware pottery and Toronto Street on the swamp adjacent to the railroad, and also on Stewart's pond in the vicinity of what is now the trailer court, and by those who disregarded parent's admonition, on the backwater below the dike at Brown's Island. This latter area was more closely restricted, when a young man named Forester plunged through the ice to his death. I can still recall his companions bringing his body up the railroad tracks on a handcar borrowed from the railroad storage shed that stood adjacent to the Abe Cheeks homestead where the steel plant stands today. However, the island was a far distant place to us, and we derived more pleasure from the action taking place in the immediate." Published by Toronto Tribune Publishing Company

Hancock County Courier, January 6, 1921 – OFFICERS MAKE BIG RAID ON BROWN'S ISLAND — "With the discovery of a large liquor cache' on Brown's Island Friday afternoon by Sheriff Armour S. Cooper and two Weirton policemen, Hancock County police authorities are confident that the hiding place and headquarters of a number of West Virginia liquor runners has been found.

"In what is considered one of the biggest raids ever conducted in this section, Sheriff Cooper and Policeman Anderson and Greenwich of the Weirton force swooped down upon the Island Friday afternoon located just below Toronto.

"In a search of the Island, the authorities discovered between 300 and 400 gallons of raisin jack and several hundred gallons of wine. In connection with the raid three men, giving their names as Gus Poplin, Gus Galutiu and Dan Populas were arrested by the police. A formal charge of hunting without a license was preferred against the men, who carried guns said the police. . . A continued search of the Island failed to locate any of the necessary equipment used in manufacture of the raisin jack or wine, leading police to believe that the Island has been used merely as a storage place."

Steubenville Herald Star, September 1, 1921 – PLANS FOR

LABOR DAY OUTING — "The big picnic on Brown's Island, Labor Day, given by the Trade & Labor Assembly will undoubtedly be one of the "big" events for which Steubenville is noted.

"All of the committees are hard at work and are meeting with unprecedented success. All of the business firms in the city, nearly, without exception, are doing everything possible to help the different committees make this the largest picnic ever held in the vicinity...There will be running races, for men, women, boys and girls. Jumping races novelty races, tug of war, etc.

"There will be dancing both on the boat and on the island, all of which will be free. There will be absolutely no charge of any kind for any amusement, as it is the endeavor to provide all with a good time at the expense of the Assembly and the wide awake business men of Steubenville.

"Brown's Island is in one of the beauty spots of the whole Ohio Valley, and anyone who has not visited this delightful spot will be repaid by doing so. No finer place could be imagined for holding a big, old time family picnic."

Hancock County Courier, August 30, 1923 – BROWN'S ISLAND CAMP IS RAIDED — "Eighteen men were jailed and arrested at Weirton charged with possession of intoxicants and 6 quarts of white whiskey and 45 cases of beer are in possession of state authorities there as a result of a raid on a camp on Brown's Island in the Ohio River near Weirton by Sheriff J.S.D. Mercer, a squad of deputies and W. Va. state troopers. The camp is said to be that of the Steubenville Rod and Gun Club and the prisoners, all of whom authorities believe gave fictitious names, are said to be prominent Steubenville residents.

Weirton Daily Times September 8, 1956 –WOMEN, Three Children Drown in Ohio Drown in Ohio After Picnic on Brown's Island

Weirton Police and Weirton Steel Safety officials began "dragging operations early this morning for the bodies of four missing persons who are believed to have drowned after a boat they were riding in upset in the Ohio River after returning to shore after Friday (September 7) afternoon picnic on Brown's Island, located in the middle of the river of the river north of the Fort Steuben Bridge.

Victims of the tragedy are reported to be.Mrs. Becky Mullens, age 47, no address. Shirley Thomas, age 10, 405 Fourth Street. Lila Jean Thomas, 7 same address as above. Kenny Mullens, age 7, no address.

Two persons, a father and son, survived the overturning. Surviving from the grim mishaps were: Chester Thomas Sr., age 46, 905 Fourth Street. Chester Thomas, Jr. age 13, same address as above.

Police first received notification of the overturning when they received a call from Kenneth Buchanan, an employee at the city filtration plant at 8:49 p.m. Buchanan reported to police that a young boy, Thomas, came in the plant and reported to police that a young boy, Thomas came to the plant and reported the upsetting of the boat. The Weirton Police quickly dispatched two patrol cars in the scene of the accident where they found the two Thomases.

The Weirton Steel Company police than sent a tug boat to assist in finding the four missing persons but failed to find any signs of the victims.

About 10:30 a.m. today the motorboat in which the victims were riding was recovered by rescue workers at the scene, from beneath the moored barges. It was assumed that the four were underneath barges.

Young Thomas gave police a report of what happened and

Merriment on the Island and Other Notable Events

told them that the six persons had gone on Brown's Island for a picnic and were returning to the West Virginia shore when, as they were nearing the boat's motor "konked out.' He said that this father tried to paddle with his hands to keep the boat from being swept downstream, however, the boat then crashed sideways into the mooring pontoon of the Weirton Steel dock and overturned.

The Thomas youth said that he scrambled into the pontoon and then assisted his father on but was unable to help any other four occupants of the boat as the swift current swept them and the boat downstream.

Attendants at Lock No. 10 were notified immediately of the accident and said that the wickets were down, however, they were on the lookout throughout the night for the victims.

They reported the river last night as being very muddy and current being very swift. A large tugboat was sent to the scene early this morning to aid in moving the large barges where the four persons are believed to be moored beneath.

Note: In an update in the Weirton Daily Times on September 12, 1956 they wrote of the recovery of the bodies. On Tuesday Shirley Thomas, 10 and Kenneth Mullins, 7, both of Weirton.

"Kenneth's body was recovered Tuesday morning about 8 miles downsteam from the sight of the accident and Shirley's body was found some 3 miles further south. Mrs. Mullins' body was recovered Monday night at the Wellsburg lock. Lila Jean's body was recovered on the day of the accident."

Chapter Twenty-One

INDUSTRIALISTS BUY THE ISLAND

Cyrus Ferguson

Cyrus Ferguson purchased Brown's Island in two parts. He acquired the northern part from Lyman Steadman in August 1918. He purchased the remaining southern portion from Harry McGinnis in November 1919. Ferguson was the first industrialist to take ownership of the 250 acres of fertile farmland, situated in the middle of the Ohio River, often described as "the most beautiful island."

Ferguson, who was of Scotch-Irish descent, was born in 1852 on the Dave Campbell farm, two miles east of Weirton. Orphaned at a young age, he ventured out on his own and worked at various farms in Hancock County.

He married Mary Elizabeth Smith in 1875. They had six children: Walter, who married Eunice Hindman; Frances, wife of James Bowers; Mary, wife of J.J. Weir; Nancy, wife of Charles Robinson; and sons Edward and Everett.

Described as "a man of exceptional foresight and business ability," he became one of the leading developers of Weirton.

Industrialists Buy the Island

In 1883 he opened a meat market in Wellsburg, West Virginia, and two years later moved to McDonald, Pennsylvania where he engaged in the manufacture of brick. He began to display his exceptional foresight when he entered the business of oil speculation in 1891. From there his fortune grew steadily.

Ferguson returned to Hancock County in 1902 and took up residence in the Crawford house at the foot of Sugar Creek Hollow. Using his profits from his oil business to buy up large tracts of land in the valley, he purchased ten farms totaling 1,700 acres "extending north of the village, between the hills to west and east, all the way to the Ohio River at the northern extend of Brown's Island. " (*History of Weirton, WV,* David Javersak, p. 68)

In 1907, he developed the Hollidays Cove Oil Field and, in the process, discovered "one of the largest Bereagrit sand oil pools ever discovered in the world." (*History of Hancock County,* Jack Welch, p. 80)

In 1909, Ferguson sold 105 acres of land to Ernest T. Weir for the construction of his new steel mill. By 1912 the growing need for housing in Weir's new town prompted Ferguson to lay out the first allotment of 160 lots "extending from Virginia Avenue to Purdy's store, which was located at Purdy's Alley and Main Street." (*History of Hancock County,* Jack Welch, p. 78) He gave free factory sites to bring in business and donated two lots for the construction of the First Christian Church at Lee Avenue and Main Street. Through his leadership he became a prominent figure in the development of the new community north of Holliday's Cove, known as Weirton.

He also was a leading force in the construction of the bridge across the Ohio River (later known as Market Street Bridge) that connects Steubenville with West Virginia. Ferguson worked with

Steubenville banker Dohrman Sinclair to bring a trolley car line across the river. The line was completed through Holliday's Cove in 1911, and by 1913 it was extended further north to Weirton.

In 1920 Ferguson sold his interests in the coal and oil industry and ventured west to Colorado. He passed away several years later in June 1926. His body was returned to the valley in which he had made his fortune. He was laid to rest in Union Cemetery in Steubenville, Ohio.

In the year prior to his death, Ferguson sold Brown's Island to his son Everett. Since the early 1900s, the island had been the scene of many community celebrations. It also held a fascination for those seeking the quiet solitude of nature and continued to flourish as "the most beautiful island."

Everett Ferguson

In April 1925 Cyrus Ferguson sold Brown's Island to his son Everett, a resident of Steubenville. Everett had inherited his father's acumen for business and was highly regarded as "one of the successful mine owners and oil operators in this section of Ohio." (*Ancestry.com. History of Ohio*)

Everett Ferguson was born in Washington County, Pennsylvania in 1879 and was educated in Pennsylvania schools. He was a graduate of McDonald High School and continued his studies at Kiski Preparatory School at Saltsburg, where he completed a general business course. Everett remained active in his father's coal and oil business until 1920 when his father sold his interests and moved to Colorado. Everett continued his involvement in the coal and oil industry independently and became head of Unity Coal Corp. He also served as director of the Steubenville Bank and Trust Company in Ohio.

In August 1906 Everett Ferguson married Emma Potter. They had one son, Everett, Jr., born August 12, 1910. During the twenty years that Ferguson owned Brown's Island, several notable –and at times tragic-- events occurred there.

In the early hours of March 22, 1932, a cargo plane carrying 47 sacks of mail and one passenger left Columbus, Ohio en route to Pittsburgh. Nearly two hours into the flight, the single engine plane lost its way in a sleet storm over Steubenville, Ohio. At 3 A.M., the ice-laden aircraft was heard flying over Weirton. The pilot struggled to regain control as he circled the valley several times, apparently looking for a place to land. It was 3:30 A.M. when the roar of the engine stopped. The plane had slammed into the southern tip of Brown's Island, killing both the pilot Hal George, a veteran aviator, and his woman passenger Dr. Carol Skinner Cole, a noted St. Louis physician. The craft went down less than a mile and a half north of the Half Moon airfield on the West Virginia side. George's body was retrieved from the tangled wreckage within hours of the crash. The body of Dr. Cole remained missing for several weeks until April 23, when it was discovered by river men near Dam No. 10 on the Ohio side at the base of Slack Street, Steubenville, Ohio the same city in which her great-grandfather had lived as an early settler.

In 1942 Weirton Steel constructed a permanent bridge across the main channel on the West Virginia side, giving the company direct access to Brown's Island. Any construction activity that may have occurred there during the 1940s most likely was confined to the north end. The densely wooded south end — which was thick with maple, oak, birch, walnut, apple, and other fruit-bearing trees, remained untouched.

In 1946, Everett Ferguson sold Brown's Island to industrialist, Michael Starvaggi, owner of Weirton Ice and Coal Supply.

Ferguson died September 1956. He is buried in Union Cemetery, Steubenville, Ohio.

Artis Monigold

"My grandfather, who I was named after, lived on the island. He lived on the island in the 1930s or just before that. Before the dams were constructed during the 50s, they had stepping stones on the north end where it was shallow that would allow you to cross over, but these were only visible on the Ohio side of the river.

"My grandfather communicated with our relatives on the Ohio side of the river with a conch shell he blew into to get their attention. This action created a real loud noise. The Monigold family on the island used skiffs to travel back and forth. It was about 100 yards over to the mainland. My grandfather drove a team of horses across the farm As far as artifacts from the Native Americans, they found arrowheads on the lower end of the island. The tribes made their flints down at the southern end of the island.

Chapter Twenty-Two

RIVER OF RAMPAGE 1936

The following account is based on local news reports, March 17-21, 1936, and the book *River on a Rampage"* by Roger Pickenpaugh.

It was a flood of many names. Some call it the "Record Flood of 1936." Others named it the "Great Potomac Flood." Still others refer to it as the "St. Patrick's Day Flood". No matter what you call it, according to the National Weather Service, it was "one of the region's worst national disasters."

Flooding began in New England on March 12 as the Penobscot and Kennebec Rivers began overflowing their banks. For the next nine days, floodwaters surged through seventeen states and the District of Columbia, leaving in its wake death and destruction. Among the places hardest hit was the Upper Ohio River Valley.

On March 17 high water began flooding the Point in Pittsburgh, where the two rivers, the Allegheny and Monongahela, meet to form the Ohio. The wealthy Triangle business district was nearly inundated with depths of 15 to 20 feet in some streets. The *Pittsburgh Post-Gazette* noted, "Great timbers, roofs of houses, [and] tree trunks whirled through the canyons of the downtown district, crashing through plate glass windows and spilling thousands of dollars' worth of merchandise into the boiling flood." On March 19 a reporter from the *Post-Gazette* toured the Triangle by boat. He described a ghastly scene of "a raw, sickly, muddy sodden lake that rippled desolation." Nearly 50,000 people in the Pittsburgh area were made homeless by the flood. Fifty-six had lost their lives.

The already swollen Ohio became a river of rampage as it surged southward toward West Virginia and Ohio. Chester, the first West Virginia town in its path, sat above the flood plain and was spared the brunt of its fury. Roger Pickenpaugh, author of *River on a Rampage,* interviewed Chester historian Roy Cashdollar. He recalls, "The flood was little more than a spectator sport. Many of the curious sat on the 'old' Chester Bridge. We saw a lot of stuff going down the river, trees and brush. Most curious was "a chicken coop with a chicken still perched atop it."

The swirling current rolled on toward New Cumberland, the Hancock County seat and a town of two levels. The lower level business section had been completely flooded and sustained heavy damage. The post office was submerged up to its roof, as was the Manas Theatre. Evart Joy's grocery store was lifted from its foundation and floated across Chester Street. The water severely damaged the furnishing of the Fred T. Bradley Funeral Home and washed forty-two caskets down the Ohio.

More than 150 families had evacuated their homes in the lower level downtown district. Many took refuge on the higher ground of Ridge Avenue. At least seven houses were washed away. It was estimated that more than 800 residents were left homeless. The *Independent* called it "one deplorable sight."

On March 18 the *Weirton Daily Times* reported that old-timer Joe Doak came down the hill from his home on Gobbler's Knob to view the swollen river. He predicted that it would be "the worst flood since the heller of '84." At 10 A.M the following day, lock number 9 reported a crest of 51.4 feet, which exceeded records of both 1884 and 1913 by five feet, ten inches.

The angry river moved swiftly toward Weirton and Holliday's Cove. First in its path was Brown's Island, a stretch of land two miles long and a half mile wide. The island stood no chance against the powerful current, as it soon was washed over and totally submerged by the rising water. Only a ghostly outline of the tallest trees could be seen. No one was living there at the time. The Arthur Holsinger family was the last family to reside on the island. In the early 1930s, they built a house on stilts and farmed a portion of the land. The Holsingers moved to the mainland in 1935. The flood had destroyed the house and other buildings, bringing to a close more than 100 years of homesteading on Brown's Island.

If good fortune could be found among the muck and misery of this terrible flood, it would be found on the high ground of Weirton, Hancock County's largest city. Because of its elevated terrain, thousands of residents had been spared the ravages of a river gone wild. Weirton Steel was the only steel plant in the region that continued to operate with no interruptions. But Holliday's Cove, Weirton's neighbor to the south in Brooke County, did not share their good fortune.

Floodwaters reached Holliday's Cove on March 18, quickly inundating the lower section of the Cove and Half Moon area. The streets hardest hit were Ferry Road, Washington, and Main. The *Weirton Daily Times* reported, "92 people were carried out of 38 homes on Washington Street and Ferry Road between 1:00 A.M. and 10:00 A.M. by a battery of volunteers." They waded through knee-deep water and carried them out on their backs until a canoe could be found.

In the lower business section of Main Street, the Crago filling station, Triangle Garage, Kuntz's Market, and Veterans of Foreign Wars were steeped in muddy water. Kusic Motors and DiNovo garages were also affected. Heavy damage was done at DiNovo's as 10 cars were submerged in the basement. Communication lines were down. The State Route 2 underpass was flooded, and the Fort Steuben Bridge linking Weirton to Steubenville was blocked. The only connection between the two cities was by rail. In the aftermath, it was reported that "mud and slime from six inches to two feet deep lay on the streets of New Cumberland and Holliday's Cove."

The muddy, murky, debris-filled water continued its rampage toward Follansbee and Wellsburg. In Follansbee two flood-related deaths were reported. Fifty-six-year-old Basale Campaign, a resident of Raymond Street, was urged to abandon his home, but he refused to leave. The next day, police used hooks to recover his body from his flooded home. A second death occurred when Joe Zwolenek, a WPA (Works Progress Administration) worker, died suddenly from "exertion and exposure" after several days of working tirelessly to aid victims in the flood zone. According to the *Wellsburg Herald,* Follansbee was flooded "from Allegheny Street, reaching out in width to some points on Jefferson Street and extending south from Allegheny to the entire length of the town." The rising floodwaters had driven at least 400 people from their homes.

Wellsburg, the Brooke County seat, was next in its path. This small, picturesque town, set snuggly between the hillside and the river, had little chance against the ever-rising river. The *Herald* reported, "Only the extreme eastern section of the city escaped the turbulent Ohio, which inundated virtually eighty percent of the community." The flood crested in Wellsburg at 54.5 feet, again surpassing the "Heller of '84" record. The business and manufacturing district was devastated. The *Herald* gave a partial list of those hardest hit: Emig Brothers, Federman-Famous Store, Johnnie's Market, Monahan Jewelry Store, Weisberger's Clothing Store, Kroger Grocery, and A & P Store. Among manufacturers, B. O. Cresap Sand and Gravel Plant, Harvey Paper Company, and Eagle Manufacturing suffered heavy losses. Hardest hit was Erskine Glass, as the facility was "almost turned into a shambles."

Roger Pickenpaugh noted in his book *River on a Rampage,* "The flood was no respecter of places of worship. The Methodist-Episcopal Church partially collapsed. Its second floor fell into the first, carrying a section of the pipe organ with it. The Baptist Church, located at Eighteenth and Charles Streets, was completely inundated. Water also entered St. John's Catholic Church."

Hundreds of residents were trapped in the upper floors of their homes waiting to be rescued. George Larrimore, a Brooke County Court attaché, worked on a rescue boat in the cold, damp air well after dark. He recounted that long terror-filled night to an Associated Press reporter. It was "the most disorganized and terrifying thing I have ever seen," he said. "Every house we passed people hung from the windows and screamed for us to come and get them. It was horrible, the noise and confusion."

On the night of March 18, the flood-stricken town suffered two tragic losses. A boat carrying five people capsized in the swirling backwater near Fifth Street and Charles. Elmer Leonard, 41, who was rowing the boat, and a three-year old girl, Marion Toner, died in the accident.

On March 19, the raging torrents of the "beautiful" Ohio rolled southward toward Wheeling. Wheeling Island lay directly in its path. Every building on this river island of 10,000 residents was flooded. Despite the evacuation order, nearly 4,000 remained in the upper floors of their homes and, in many cases, without heat, electricity, food, or drinking water. A reporter for the *Wheeling News,* who lived on the island, described scenes of desolation and terror. "Everything is covered up," he said. "Over on Wheeling Island, the place is deluged and people are trying to escape the danger in the upper floors. The Gospel Tabernacle over there was carried away and crashed against a drug store and the pier of a bridge. There are a couple of houses tumbling against the Tabernacle. Maybe one of them is mine." A fleet of motor boats was dispatched quickly in an effort to rescue the stranded from second-floor windows.

Early in the day of March 17, the south end of Wheeling proper began to flood. Water crept over Main Street at Sixteenth and by evening had reached Market Street, "the heart of Wheeling's great business district." On March 19 it was reported that water had reached a depth of 15 feet on Market Street and "businesses were under water up to the first-floor ceilings. Hundreds were marooned in the structures."

Thousands of flood victims, aided by the Red Cross, were taken to the Market Auditorium. On March 20 an Associated Press reporter captured the scene of despair. The auditorium was home to "some 4,000 of the city's homeless and sick, huddled in little knots, murmuring and weeping," he wrote. "Children in mud-caked clothing wandered around, wide-eyed and dazed, many seeking parents they would never find. Everywhere the sick and aged lay still on hard cots." The Red Cross estimated that 6,700 families had been driven from their homes with little more than what possessions they could carry.

The record-shattering crest of 54.5 feet came on March 19 at 2:00 P.M the Wheeling Wharf. Flood stage was 36. The *Steubenville*

Herald Star reported 17 flood-related deaths in Wheeling. An estimated 27,000 were left homeless.

Flood-stricken communities on the Ohio side — East Liverpool, Wellsville, Empire, Stratton, Steubenville, Mingo, Brilliant, and Martins Ferry — suffered the same hardships of terror-filled nights, homelessness, deprivation, and the ever-present threat of disease. WPA nurses worked with doctors in Jefferson County to inoculate 2,500 victims from contagious fevers.

Through the resilience of nature and strength of the human spirit, nearly all of the flood-torn places on both sides of the river, including Brown's Island, would eventually recover from their devastating losses. The 1936 flood of many names had left its mark throughout the Upper Ohio River Valley. It would be remembered here simply for what it was — the Greatest Flood of the Century.

Chapter Twenty-Three

MICHAEL STARVAGGI IN PURSUIT OF THE AMERICAN DREAM

In 1946 Weirton industrialist and philanthropist Michael Starvaggi purchased Brown's Island from Everett Ferguson for $40,000. Starvaggi, commonly known as "Mike," was founder and chairman of the board of Starvaggi Industries. He died in 1979 at the age of 84 and left behind a legacy of community giving.

In 1913, at the age of seventeen, Starvaggi arrived in the United States from Italy with just five dollars in his pocket. Alone and unable to speak the English language, he stepped off the boat in New York Harbor and made his way to Weirton, West Virginia, where he joined his aunt Rosalie Ballato on September 5, 1913. That was the beginning of his relentless pursuit of the American Dream.

The *Weirton Daily Times*, August 8, 1979, gave the following account of hit impressive rise from "rags to riches."

"His first job was with the Weirton Steel Company, where he carried water to thirsty steelworkers. However, his independent nature quickly emerged, and he left Weirton Steel to open a small grocery and fruit store in the north end of Weirton, specializing in Italian foods. With the addition of a horse and wagon, his store

Michael Starvaggi in Pursuit of the American Dream

became a traveling vegetable and fruit market throughout the lanes and byways of Weirton.

It was not long before he added ice in the summer and coal in the winter to his inventory, and his venture soon resulted in the founding of the Weirton Ice and Coal Company. After a few years, he purchased his first bus and created the Pittsburgh and Weirton Bus Company.

As years passed, Mr. Starvaggi became the owner of the Weirton Construction Company, Steubenville Bus Company, Cove Hill Coal Company, Glenn Brooke Coal Company, and Half Moon Coal Company. He also founded the Starvaggi Charities, Inc. In 1968 all of the businesses controlled by Mr. Starvaggi were merged into the present Starvaggi Industries, Inc. and the companies remained divisions of the Industries.

Starvaggi's success in business was not without its setbacks. On a peaceful Sunday morning, April 29, 1951, a P&W Company bus, owned by Starvaggi, carrying 60 church-bound passengers lost its brakes while descending Weirton Heights Hill on Pennsylvania Avenue. The Spring 2004 issue of *Goldenseal* magazine gave a vivid account of what happened next "The runaway vehicle raced into the tight curve near the P&W garage at a speed of 50 mph. Workers inside the garage heard the horn blowing and the scream of tires. A thunderous noise followed and the building shook. The left front of the bus struck the concrete retaining wall at an angle, crushing its steel frame into a mass of twisted metal." The driver, Joe Kraina, and 12 others died in the crash. Nearly all who perished lived on Weirton Heights within one mile of each other. Seven funerals—five at St. Paul's church and two at Sacred Heart of Mary—were held in one day. The grief-stricken town mourned openly as "the streets were lined with mourners with tear-stained faces." Most of the victims were buried in the St. Paul cemetery on Weirton Heights.

In the lawsuits that followed, Starvaggi"s bus company was cleared of any wrongdoing. The judge instead shifted blame to the bus manufacturer, General Motors, for their faulty design of the braking system.

Through his unstoppable rise to success, Starvaggi had captured his American Dream of building a commercial empire. The *WV State Journal*, June 22, 2012 edition stated, "Still in operation today, Starvaggi Industries has extensive real estate holdings along with a river terminal, a storage division, coal operations, a trucking and trucking equipment operation, and ready-mix concrete division."

Starvaggi was known for his generous gifts. He donated land for the construction of Madonna High School, St. Joseph School, and St. Joseph Church. He also donated a 22-acre tract for the construction of Weirton Medical Center. In addition, he provided equipment, material, and funding for the Gilson Avenue Fire Station. The College of Steubenville, now Franciscan University, received a grant of $125,000 for the construction of a new campus building, which bears the Starvaggi name.

Although he and his wife Angeline had no children, they showed great concern for local youth by donating reclaimed land for the termite and little league baseball fields. He and his wife also donated the Starvaggi Memorial Pool and park to the citizens of Weirton. Most generous, however, was Mike's personal gift of $200,000 toward the construction of the Hancock County Children's Home.

Starvaggi expressed his love for his new country many times. In an editorial published in the *Sunday News Register*, August 12,

1979, he said, "All the things I have done are a small part of my appreciation for everything this country has done for me. All of us who came from Italy or any foreign country should thank God for giving us the privilege to come here and enjoy this great country. It may sound funny to some, but America is Heaven. It's as simple as that."

Despite his wealth, Mike remained a "common man" whose hard work and determination, mixed with kindness and generosity, made him an uncommon success. Through the years, Starvaggi received many honors for his charitable works. He was inducted into the Lou Holtz Hall of Fame in 1999 and was chosen again as an inductee to the Weirton Hall of Fame in 2009. In the Lou Holtz ceremony, he was lauded for "taking great care and pride in restoring strip-mined land to a condition that was good or better than when he went in." As a result of his good works, he was named "Father of Reclamation in West Virginia" in 1978 by West Virginia University and the West Virginia Surface Mine Association.

Brown's Island had retained its pristine association and continued to attract fun-seekers and lovers of nature. In 1957 Starvaggi sold Brown's Island to National Steel Corp. for $42,000. The transaction brought an end to the island's agricultural era and ushered in the destructive forces of industrial growth.

Michael Starvaggi was just one of the many immigrants that came to the Ohio Valley as Weirton Steel grew and welcomed "many nationalities from Europe, plus some from the Middle East, as well as a large number of African-Americans." According to Michael Javersak, in a *West Virginia Encyclopedia* from Weirton. The town hosted parades celebrating the variety of ethnic groups coming to the area. This Festival of Nations has been revitalized recently in Weirton as an annual event that displays crafts, food, and entertainment to highlight various cultural traditions. So, the new immigrants came to the steel mills and Weirton's population had increased to 18,000 residents by 1940. Steubenville had close to 38,000 inhabitants. Most of the immigrants came during the period from 1880 to 1920 with 4 million Italians migrating to the United States.

Chapter Twenty-Four

REBUILDING AND TAKEOVERS

It took about five months to repair the battery after the explosion. The workers showed motivation to get this job completed. The main area of destruction was confined to an area around 50 feet wide and 30 feet long, according to an article in the *Pittsburgh Press* printed December 17, 1972. Other buildings may have had foundation issues from the impact of the explosion. *The Pittsburgh Post-Gazette* reporters wrote, "The powerful explosion, centered in a chamber-like basement area beneath the ovens, caved in brick walls, ripped out steel reinforcements and shook buildings in downtown Weirton, two miles away."

Koppers Company, already behind schedule, worked to get the plant functioning as soon as possible. Never having experienced a tragedy like this in its sixty-five years of building coke plants, Koppers began work several days after the accident to build bypasses of the damaged area. An article in the *Pittsburgh Post-Gazette* said, "one official estimated total damage would amount to millions of dollars."

In August of 1982, after nine years of operation, the coke plant on Brown's Island shut down, laying off or reassigning 275 workers. The "coke plant of the future" operated a little more than nine years. One worker reported that while he was on the island, management had briefly talked of adding to the coke plant. They abandoned the idea once the steel mills started faltering.

After World War II, Japan and Europe had to rebuild their steel factories, which they located close to raw materials and the market. These countries upgraded to Basic Oxygen Steelmaking in their new innovations, and the foreign countries made it cheaper with lower labor costs. For example, Japanese mills paid their workers 23 percent less than U.S. steel mills. The foreign mills improved their technology as they built their new mills. In the 1970s the U.S. steel industry faltered. In 1977 fourteen major steel mills closed. Layoffs occurred across the American steel industry.

Steel companies added other products, even taking on banking to their holdings. The 1980s brought a shocking change to Weirton Steel when in March 1982, National Steel said they would no longer keep Weirton Steel open unless they could find a buyer. When no buyers came forth, Weirton Steel's workers formulated a plan to buy the plant in an innovative ESOP (Employee Stock Ownership Plan). The individual steelworkers would give up some of their pay to put into renovations for the mill to be viable. Each worker gave up a third of his/her wages and joined management in producing a high-quality steel at a lower price.

The workers began fundraising in the community by having food fairs, telethons, and celebrity fundraisers. The community participated in these events and workers in the town enjoyed a sense of solidarity.

By September of 1983, the employees received a document of disclosure and attended meetings so that they could understand their responsibilities. Media showed up on the day of the vote as this would be the largest employee-owned company in the country at this time. The employees voted in favor of the plan by about 86 percent. Robert Loughhead took over the helm at Weirton Steel Company.

In Jack Welch's reprint of *History of Hancock County*, he describes the reaction of the town after the January 11, 1984 signing. "Following the signing a celebration was held in the Milsop Community Center, which was attended by 1500 people. The centerpiece of the celebration was a 200-pound, 16-foot marble cake with 26 layers (arranged in 17 stacks). Created by Mickey Weyrauch, Manager of Royal Pastry, the cake was a gift to ESOP. Members of the Weirton Woman's Club and the Weir High Band performed."

For several years the ESOP plan was successful. At the end of 1986, employees received their first profit sharing check of around $2500. Under Bob Loughhead's management, the earning for Weirton Steel showed good profits. From 1984 to 1987, the mill's income totaled over $247 million (before profits were shared out). Towards the end of the decade, the mill needed renovation. In 1986 management discussed whether to keep importing continuous-cast slabs from Germany or build a new caster. Costs would be high, to the tune of 150-200 million dollars.

Some of the board members, however, wished to ease out Bob Loughhead. Bob Loughhead retired in 1987, and Herb Elish took over the reins. A few more profitable years followed, and the mill still employed eight thousand workers. However, profits eventually turned into staggering losses: $230 million in 1993; $320 million in 2001; and almost $700 million in 2003. Job losses followed with around five thousand employees losing their jobs. Especially brutal for workers was a stock collapse where stock values dipped from over fourteen dollars to just a few cents.

While workers suffered the brunt of the collapse, executives raised their salaries and protected themselves from the consequences of their actions. Only three positions on the board were filled by workers. Author John D. Russell coined the term about this tragedy, saying "there is no "we" in Weirton." Several local authors wrote books about what happened to Weirton Steel.

Russell also noted, "Weirton failed because of anarchy in the domestic and global markets, a downturn in U.S. economic activity 1990 to 1994, and then more crucially, the final crises in Southeast Asia (1997) and the U.S.S.R. (1998). Together with an overvalued dollar, these crises caused a flood of imports and a collapse in the price of steel to historic lows that wiped out slender operating margins"and handing over pensions to the PBGC (Pension Benefit Guaranty Corporation) for the retired steelworkers. ISG had previously bought other faltering mills including LTV, Bethlehem Steel and Acme Metals. With the purchase of Weirton Steel, they became the "largest steel producer in North America." Wilber Ross, founder of ISG, owned one third of the company's stock. In 2003 he made about 777 million on his personal holdings and investment funds.

Meanwhile, the workers who had given up wages to finance their company lost all their stock funds. Retirees who had been promised money when they collected Social Security lost that benefit. Also, they would have to finance their health care. The men who dedicated a great portion of their time to the mill, some sacrificing their lives, and others suffering health problems from exposure to toxic and carcinogenic substances, again saw their promised benefits go up in smoke.

In April 2005 Mittal gave $4.5 billion in cash and stock to buy out ISG. Mittal began by temporarily downing the blast furnace and laying off about 750 workers. By November, they decided to close the blast furnaces and other furnaces permanently. The cost of transporting iron ore and importing coke was hurting profits. Mittal Steel joined with Arcelor and the former Weirton Steel became Arcelor Mittal in 2006. This merger would make Mittal the largest steel company in the world. Two years later Arcelor Mittal closed the hot mill. More pieces of the mill came down, including the Basic Oxygen Plant, reheating furnaces, and Brown's Island.

Eslich Wrecking Company from Columbus, Ohio, a third-generation family business, took on the job of tearing down the coking facility on Brown's Island. In a 2010 brochure, the Brown's Island plant demolition was listed as their largest job at that time. The 40-acre clear out took a year and a half to complete and they "removed the coke ovens, the crushers that crushed the coke, smokestacks, storage bin and adjacent buildings."

In the beginning of February 2017, Arcelor Mittal sold 1100 acres of their property to Frontier Group, a brownfield developer company based in Buffalo, New York.

Some companies stayed on the island after the coke plant closed. IMS (International Mill Services) was one. Writers of the Rahall report wrote, "Further south was an active slag processing operation. The slag processing took place on land owned by Weirton Steel and leased to International Mill Services (IMS). IMS received waste slag from the mill, processed the slag and shipped out the finished product by truck and barge primarily for use in the construction industry. The barge loading facility at IMS was an example of a privately owned special purpose terminal, useful for loading processed slag into barges.

Starvaggi also did some work on the island. Chuck Ballato remembers performing a variety of jobs on the island. "I got all the jobs nobody else wanted to do. I worked for three and a half years on the island on behalf of Starvaggi Industries. Some of the work I did included operating mobile equipment and loading coke trucks." Other companies not listed here also occupied the island. People who worked on the island after the explosion tell their stories in the next chapter.

Chapter Twenty-Five
LATER WORKERS TELL THEIR STORIES

Tom Zielinsky

Tom Zielinsky remembers the day of the 1972 explosion. "I was driving up to see my mom and dad in New Cumberland. While crossing the King's Creek Bridge, I heard the loud sound created by the blast. When I got to my parents' house, they had their transistor radio on in the kitchen, and we listened to the news of the explosion."

Tom worked on the mainland and provided the procedures of coking and a list of positions available to men who worked in the coke plant. These same positions would be at the new battery but with new automation tools. The training would have been different because the men could operate equipment from a remote control. They would have a harness on and walk beside the equipment with their control.

"Coal car dumper operator—operated the dumper car used to dump the coal cars. Coal is automatically moved by conveyer to the top of each coke battery and stored for the 'larry cars.'

"Larryman—operated the 'larry car.' These cars were loaded with coal and would fill the oven after the coke was pushed out.

"Pusher--pusher machine would remove the doors and then push the coke from one side of the battery through the oven to a waiting dump car. The dump car then went to the quench tower/ for a water bath to begin cooling the coke.

"Quench operator--once the hot coke entered the quench tower/station, a large amount of water was poured on the coke to stop the heating process and allow the coke to cool.

"Coke car dump car operator--the dump car would take the pushed coke from the battery to the cooling tower/station for a water bath. Once quenched with water the car would travel back to the dumping area where the coke would be dumped onto a conveyor belt and moved to a storage area for complete cooling.

"The screen man operated the screening station. This person would make sure all coke was properly sized and extra-large pieces were positioned to be broken into smaller, more acceptable size pieces. The nozzleman cleaned the ports for air and cleaned or replaced the nozzles on the batteries."

Mr. Zielinsky had some comments on a valve suffering breakage. He discussed how soot markings on the valve would indicate what had happened to the valve. If the crack was in the valve the markings would be on the valve. If the seam were blown apart the soot would be outside the valve.

Tom remarked that after the coke plant closure, some acids and remnants from the island were dumped at the Shiloh Landfill close to Woodview golf course. This landfill closed six or seven years ago.

Tom Zielinsky has written several books on local history. "As for my books, the first was, *"The Final Days of Weirton Steel," Could the collapse have been prevented?* This was published in 2010. It captured the last five years of happenings before the bankruptcy. Next, 2017,*"Rockyside, A Forgotten Mining Community'*. It describes the clay mining and brick making operations both north and south of New Cumberland, but specifically the mining community of Rockside, sitting on a barren hillside, north of New Cumberland, from 1870 to 1950. In 2020,*"Zalia, Hancock County, West Virginia, Rediscovering a lost community."* This book specifically describes the mining community of Zalia, which was located just south of New Cumberland, from 1832 to around 1975. Both books about the mining communities captures some of the families and happenings during this period of time. Finally, my last book, 2021, is a redo of the first Weirton Steel book. The *2nd Edition* of «*The Final Days of Weirton Steel,*» brings the reader up to date on events surrounding the mill and the community of Weirton, since 2010. This time in newer print, edited corrections, and colored pictures."

Charles Leonard

"I worked in the new coke ovens inside the very basement where men lost their lives! All the older employees would try to scare me with haunted stories of the screams from the men who had died. Even though it was kept spotless and vented in the basement, most new employees there experienced an eerie feeling, and everybody in their hearts thought so, even if they didn't speak about it. I will never forget it.

"In my job as a laborer, I did lots of clean up and any other work that needed done. My job did not pay well. I entered by the West Virginia side through Gate 1. Back then if you lived in Ohio, you had to use the tiny bridge on the Ohio side, but since I lived in West Virginia, I used the big steel bridge. A lot of people didn't know that the bridge was made of pure steel and had two wide lanes. The bridge outsized the railroad bridge south of the new Fort Steuben Bridge (Veterans Bridge). It sits way up in the air.

"When I worked on Brown's Island, it didn't require a lot of manpower to run the coke ovens. Maybe thirty people. A couple of laborers worked each shift in case they needed them to do something. Extra laborers were called in on special days when the furnaces were down or there was an emergency clean up. The mill made sure we kept busy, even if we were one of the two on the shifts when the coke ovens ran. The new ovens were kept exceptionally clean and in good working order, especially when compared to the old ovens on the mainland.

"I graduated from Brooke High in 1975. My career with Weirton Steel began in October 1978 and lasted close to twenty years. I was one of the first to go as not too many people had less time than I did. When I worked on the island, the only safety equipment I wore was my shoes, helmet, gloves, and a paper white mask that covered my mouth and nose. I had two lockers, one for clean clothes and one for dirty clothes in buildings all over the mill. I labored in many places of the mill. The only places I never worked were in the General Office buildings and the Half Moon area. I kept keys to all the different locks because when I first started to work, I never knew to what department I would be assigned.

"I would work better jobs when people went on vacations, but I basically spent my time in the labor gangs throughout the mill. Management laid me off for almost five years, and I lost my recall rights. Five years later, the union took the matter to court, and I got my years back, but no pay. My wife and I had our dream house picked out, but she became sick with heart problems, and I spent three and a half years taking care of her. I never did buy a new house.

James "Jumbo" Panacci

This interview was from an article published in *Goldenseal* in 1987 by Jane Kraina

Weirton prides itself on its rich ethnic culture. Immigrants moved to the area in the early 1900s because of the employment the steel mills offered. Many Italians came and they and other European groups formed a community of close-knit families. James "Jumbo" Panacci, the son of immigrant parents comes from this background.

Panacci wrestled as a youth and said his muscles earned him his unusual nickname. He claims he shrank in the army, but the name stuck. Jumbo and his wife "Minnie" have three children. Two of their children still live at home, and a married son lives in the same street. Such closeness is typical of Weirton.

Jumbo Panacci labored in the Weirton Steel mill for 42 years and worked on Browns Island from the time the coke plant moved to the island in the early 1970's until he retired in 1981. He monitored the temperature in the ovens. He worked afternoon turn the day the coke plant exploded and later served as a pallbearer for one of the workers who died in the accident.

In a recent interview, Jumbo talked of his work on the island. "My job at the mill consisted of keeping track of the temperature in the ovens," he explained. "The temperature had to be kept at a certain degree, about 2,100 degrees. If it got too low more gas had to be added."

"We drove onto the island on a bridge from the mainland," he said, "I worked all three shifts—daylight, which was eight to four; afternoon, which was four to twelve, and midnight, which was twelve to eight. We came in an hour earlier than scheduled because getting dressed to work around the ovens was no easy task. "First, we put on long johns," he elaborated. "Over them, we wore an asbestos suit which was quite heavy. We had to take off all our rings, watches and chains because they got too hot. Also, we had to put on a green respirator mask. It connected with a tube which drew dust into a box. The box was numbered. Every day we turned our box in and the mill sent the box to Pittsburgh where OSHA measured the dust in our box. We had to wear goggles or safety glasses to protect our eyes, and a safety helmet and an asbestos hood went over our heads. All our clothes got quite dirty."

Minnie attests to the dirt. "It took two days of soaking to clean his clothes," she said.

"We always had to have our safety equipment on," her husband continued. "If we were caught without it, we got three days off work without pay. The piece of equipment that bothered the men the most was the respirator mask. The tubing would get caught up in things. It was not uncommon for workers to rip them off and toss them."

Depending on their job, workers might have to wear even more protective gear. "People who worked on the battery (of coke ovens) also had to wear wooden shoes to protect their feet from the heat," Jumbo noted.

"Teamwork was very important on Browns Island," he added. "I worked with an assistant heater, heater helper and another helper."

The Browns Island team was responsible for transforming coal into coke, a high-carbon fuel, while capturing the related by-products. "The amount of material used in the coking process were quite large," according to Jumbo. "It took 32,000 pounds of coal to make 5,000 pounds of coke. The byproducts of coke were gas, tar and benzyl." Coal was trucked from the mainland on the same bridge the workers used in coming to work.

"To cool off the hot coke, the coke was pushed into a quenching or cooling car" Jumbo said. "The amount of water used to cool the coke in the quenching car was 50,000 gallons. The water was pumped in from the Ohio River."

The big industrial plant never quite overwhelmed the natural island, Jumbo said, "The coke plant took up about half the island. The rest of the island was wooded and there was a sizable deer population on the island. Sometimes the labor gang would find stones they believed to be Indian relics."

The veteran employee vividly recalls the horrible explosion of 1972, but also has many pleasant memories of his years of his years on Browns Island. That's where he acquired the family dog, from a fellow employee who had more pups than he could handle. When he learned that the fellow was contemplating dropping them off the bridge, Jumbo Panacci slipped one home to Minnie.

"One day I woke up and a puppy was in a box in the corner of my kitchen," she said. "We called him 'Meatball' because that's exactly what size he was. We had Meatball for 16 years. He finally died of a heart attack."

Bill Whanger

Bill Whanger tells his story to Jane Kraina about differences between mainland and island byproducts production.

"I worked on the mainland byproducts (BP), before the building of the coking and by products facilities on the island. I would get pulled over to the island to work in the BP control room. Men would hang out in the control room because it was air conditioned, and they could smoke in there. Byproducts consist of useful materials such as secondary light oil, secondary and intermediate, and sulfur tar driven off by coke making. The mill would sell these items to other companies. We placed tar onto a barge. They gave us a 2-way radio to communicate with the Coast Guard when loading. On the mainland men dumped sludge into old strip mines.

"The mainland BP allowed for dangerous gases to be released into the air. Chemicals being used were ammonia sulfate, pure sulfuric acid, and caustic soda for dilution and neutralization of oil. I remember the men had to be careful when looking up because the acids, such as lime and caustic acid, would disperse droplets into the air that would come down and burn their eyes. Smelling benzole made the men feel dizzy and drunk-like. The xylol and tylol also affected people. For some reason, every six months they would take blood samples from us and send them to a lab in California.

"I recall a college kid coming to work for the summer who was knocked out by hydrogen sulfur gas on the island. Inhaling too much of this gas can kill a person.

"Another danger, of course, was fire. If the fire heating the tanks was not controlled properly, 189 pounds of steam would be added to prevent an explosion. Steam had to be used to purge

Later Workers Tell Their Stories

the gas out. Tank railroad cars would be steamed out. Samples of xylol would be sent to the lab to be tested. If they were contaminated, it could ruin the whole tank.

"One night we were looking out at the sky and thinking what a beautiful sunset. It ended up being a fire at the tin mill. In the BP we took care of our own fires. We had five fire pumps. The city water pumps were white, and the Ohio River pumps were yellow.

"As the tanks on the mainland aged, rust became a problem. One dreaded job was climbing the phenol tower. Men would climb up 80 feet on ladders and the rust on the rungs would come off. Men walked on the catwalks and stairwells, so they wouldn't have to climb. Also, on the 500,000-gallon tar tank the rust was so bad you could see right through it. The top fell in. The sulfuric acid lines would sometimes leak.

"Horse manure was spread around the tanks to keep valves from freezing. The rats liked it and would scamper around in the mixture and build nests. One time a worker threw an M80 into a spot he saw a rat, and instead of a rat, a cat came staggering out.

"On the island, the gases were contained, and you didn't have to work with the sulfuric acid. There was a sulfur plant on the island. Some of the main jobs on the BP division, were foreman operator, sulfur man, bug man, light oil man, engineer, and car loader. Chemists worked on the island trying to develop new methods to break down the byproducts. They researched bugs (bacteria) that would feed on the phenol. If the phenol wasn't removed, it would make water taste bad. The EPA didn't want the phenol dumped into the river. The bug man's job was to stir the material and monitor the bug tank. The Ph had to be measured. Note: In WSX bulletin, the biological oxidation plant was called "the bacteria cafeteria."

"For some reason, the tar on the island would solidify more easily than on the mainland. It was a different consistency, and it wouldn't keep liquid like it should. One time when the company cleaned the tar tank, the tar oozed out, and they said it could be used on the island road and the cars sank in the tar.

"The island had a lot of controls that would set off alarms if different measurements were not correct. The room contained about 44 alarms and if something was wrong, they would set off an aial. The panel board had a lot of gauges and switches, and you could see which valves were open and closed on your coke gas line. This con was a problem. Before the island plants were built, the mainland used a steam whistle to communicate warnings. Two long and two short whistles meant for everyone to come.

"Four alarms served to signal the electricians and so on. On the island they switched to an intercom system which was easier to hear. One time a message came from the intercom, saying, 'It's all over.' This was rather frightening, but the warning left out one word: tar. The tar had leaked out all over.

"Air tanks were available for the men similar to what fireman use after working around some of the dangerous gases. They kept the tanks in the control room. Five-minute cans were also issued.

"In my years in the mill, I saw a lot of changes. Working amongst chemicals and fire could make for dangerous conditions, but I am still here in my nineties to tell the stories."

The Weirton Area Museum and Cultural Center

To view items from the former Weirton Steel Company, the Weirton Area Museum and Cultural is worth a visit. They have badges of older steel workers and old badges may be purchased.

They display the wooden shoes men wore in the mill and have cans that the mill produced. They have holdings from the town of Weirton and earlier Holliday's Cove.

They have made video presentations that can be purchased. A well made video is "Rediscovering Holliday's Cove which has information on Brown's Island.

Chapter Twenty-Six
OUTLOOK

Ella Jennings from Weirton was the reporter in a West Virginia Public Broadcasting feature produced in 2019 entitled "What Happened to Weirton?" Her story began with the planned implosion of the Basic Oxygen Plant on March 9, 2019. As she witnessed the fall of the BOP, she said, "Lights flashed across the rusted structure, followed by a blanketing of noise that enveloped the hillside. The BOP fell forward, unleashing a huge cloud of dust that sped towards the neighborhood below. A giant pile of sheet metal and structural beams was all that remained of what was once called 'the Mill of the Future.'"

Weirton was just one of many small towns across America affected by the decline of manufacturing, leaving many to wonder what would happen to their beloved town. Steelworkers, who once were able to provide for their families and buy them extras, faced pensions half the size expected. Their health care was gone.

Ms. Jennings was the daughter of Burt Jennings, who worked in the BOP for a year and then served as a firefighter in the mill for ten years from 1994 until 2004. She moved to Weirton in 2005 until she left for college. She was eager to leave, but on this return she learned to understand the area more.

Outlook

The workers interviewed by Ella echoed the theme of the brotherhood concept introduced earlier in this book. Crews depended on the actions of their coworkers.

Larry Tice began working for Weirton Steel in 1973 in the red-hot heat of the BOP, which motorists noticed as they passed. Larry's wife Mary told of the closeness of the workers whose lives depended on each other.

"When he trained workers, he emphasized the undivided attention needed for the job." There were mill 120 men who died on the job.

Mary added, "They were all very close-knit and ...they knew how to depend on each other. They knew what each one was capable of doing...that solidified a bond I can't even imagine." When Larry's world turned upside down with the loss of his job, he became depressed and eventually committed suicide.

When Ella Jennings went downtown, the workers at the Weir Cove Taxi said they noted the economic downturn in the area. Small businesses disappeared from downtown. One woman was happy about the reduction in bars but also lamented the diminishing of church congregations.

Because the mill had provided jobs and security for so long, the area stayed committed to the company. National Steel had branched out. "National went from the fourth-largest steel company in the country to the fourth-largest savings and loan institution." In 1982 they decided not to invest in Weirton Steel anymore. The Employee Stock Ownership Plan presented to the workers allowed the employees to buy the mill, and Weirton Steel became the new company name in 1984. In only fifteen years, 5,000 workers remained, and workers traveled to Washington, DC in 1999 to rally "for protectionist policies for the steel industry." President

Bush took the biggest stand for the steel industry three years later when he instated tariffs on steel imports in 2002.

Ms. Jennings also interviewed business leaders. When she talked to Pat Ford, he worked for the Business Development Corporation acting as a regional entity promoting industries to bring their businesses to the northern panhandle.

A Jefferson County group had a similar purpose. Their unity preserved over 7500 jobs in the area. Two hundred of the jobs produced employment for those in the natural gas industry. They use a fracking process involving digging down into the earth to blast rocks with a high-pressure water mix. After the rock is fractured, the gas and oil will flow to the well.

Frontier has sold off pieces of the mill but has kept Brown's Island. Pat Ford now works for Frontier. David Franjoine is the CEO of the Frontier Group of Companies. They have reopened docks to tether barges that carry products such as sand and gravel, gypsum, methanol, pig iron, ferro silicon, and ferro chrome. Industry Terminal and Salvage has signed on to operate the port facility. Their president, Brad Busatto, hopes to have 100 slots for barges. Busatto said in the article of the planned facility, "It will revitalize a 100-mile stretch of the Ohio River."

In an article from *The Weirton Daily Times* on August 5, 2021, written by Craig Howell, he notes that "an access road should be constructed in 2022. Frontier will update the rail line, and plans include a 500-acre industrial park for Frontier Crossings."

A Boat Trip Around the Island

In 2020 we were privileged to be taken by boat around the island by John Nodianis. He related to Mary Zwierzchowski his 40 years of experience on Griffith Island. Griffith sits close to Brown's Island, but it is much smaller. "My wife Teri and I began boating on the river in 1977, about the same time that our twin boys, Kevin and Kris, were born. That's when I bought my first boat, a 16 ft. open bow runabout. We joined the Weirton Marina in 1978. The boys grew up on the river. They learned swimming and water-tubing at an early age.

"For all the years we've been boating there, I've never been on Brown's Island. The new coke plant was operating then, and security was tight. There was no place to dock, so we went to Griffith Island several yards west of Brown's near the south end. We built four docks—two on one side and two on the other. Tim and Angela Reinard shared the island docks, Tim on one side and I on the other. Two or three other families camped there also. We brought in gas grills, picnic tables, and lawnmowers. We cleared away the weeds and planted grass, and kept the grass cut.

"The kids swam a lot and skied with inner tubes. There was a rope swing on the island. It was exciting to watch as they would swing out over the river and then let go into the water. We made them wear lifejackets. They had lots of fun.

"Kris liked to throw potato chips on the water and watch the carp come up and grab them. On one occasion, Teri and I watched a very large bird—it may have been an eagle—swoop down on the water. It came up with a carp in its mouth then flew west toward the Ohio side. We found mollusk shells in the shallow water around upper Griffith, nearly as big as my hand.

"Actually, there were two islands—upper and lower Griffith. We called the lower one Sandy Island because when you walked on it you would just sink into the sand. Upper Griffith was a mix of both sand and gravel. Sandy Island slowly disappeared when

Dravo Corporation began dredging there. They dredged around the island to the point where it eventually sank into the river." Others believe its disappearance was caused by a flood. In any event, this small river oasis, lush with green, had earned its title as the 'missing isle.'

"There were many times when we pitched tents on upper Griffith and camped overnight . We would gather driftwood from the shoreline and dry it out. Then we would make a fire ring, light a blazing campfire, and roast marshmallows.

"The following morning, we would go back to the clubhouse at the marina and clean up a bit, then return to the island, where we brewed coffee and made breakfast. We had a two-burner propane stove.

"In the summer of 2010, the good times on Griffith abruptly came to an end. "That's when someone came along and tore out our docks. We don't know who did it or why, and I don't know who owned the island at the time. They kicked us off the island and posted a No Trespassing sign. We tried to find a suitable place to rebuild, but it just never worked out. After that, we would cruise the river until we found a safe place to drop anchor and swim."

Sadly, Teri passed away in the winter of 2019, leaving behind a family tradition that continues. John explains, "We still go there. When the boys visit, they bring their kids down to the marina — Kevin with Rylan and Ashlynn, and Kris with Anne and Ben — and now they, too, have fun on the river."

In a nostalgic look back, John recounts those 40 summers of pleasure-boating near Brown's Island. "We made a lot of friends over the years. I would never have stayed with it that long if Teri hadn't liked it so much. We had good times." Of the many days — and nights — they spent camping on Griffith, he says, "Those were the best."

Conclusions

When we toured the island's area with John, people were boating close to Brown's Island, and young boys were getting ready to swing on a rope. When we passed across the island on the side that faces Ohio, I could imagine Dorothy art rowing her little boat to the shore. I thought of the thousands of people who walked on the island. I imagined Meriwether Lewis struggling with his keelboat and pirogue over the sandbars with the fish visible in the shallow water. The island was such a small place with so much history. For a piece of land that was considered unremarkable by our first president George Washington, it ended up having an impressive, colorful history. Did the long-ago natives predict the sadness of the future? One wonders. The day we visited the island, an eagle flew above the area just as it had in the past.

It is wistful to think of it as a natural place to relax, with maple trees to tap and apples for the picking. However, like much of America, heavy industrial companies have taken their toll with their depletion of resources and scarring of the land. For many in the Upper Ohio Valley, the manufacturing jobs paid well. These jobs allowed those that came to the area to send their children to college and to go on vacations. Even if enterprises could revitalize the region, the future economy would likely never supply 10,000 jobs as in the past. There are towns and other islands down the Ohio River suffering the same uninspiring economic future.

— Jane Kraina

From all appearances, Frontier Group, the current owner of Brown's Island, has made great strides in revitalizing the former Weirton Streel properties, creating a brighter outlook for the Weirton Community. In an article published in the *Brooke Review* May 1, 2020, officials of Frontier Group announced plans "to construct a 40 megawatt solar farm on Brown's Island and will include, 118,000 to 120,000 solar panels with an estimated cost of $41 million." After four decades of idled industry on the island construction of this green energy project, if it should occur, would bring a resurgence of activity back to this once-thriving manufacturing site.

From a vantage point on a wooded hillside high above the mist, overlooking the winding Ohio River, there is a glimmer of hope that someday this beleaguered island will once again be transformed from a paradise destroyed to a paradise restored.

And why not? After all, it is still a place where eagles soar.

— Mary Zwierzchowski

EPILOGUE

Secrets in the Mist is the culmination of a five-year journey of research, interviews, and writing of Brown's Island's past from its Native American roots to the present. Published in 2022, it marks the 50th anniversary of the fateful 1972 coke plant explosion and serves to honor the 19 men who lost their lives on that tragic day. We hope our efforts have brought to light many of the secrets that long been hidden in the island mist.

It is our hope that Secrets in the Mist will serve to enlighten and encourage the readers to learn more about the history of Brown's Island. We look forward to the day when a permanent memorial will be created to list the names of the 19 men who perished in the 1972 explosion. Their ultimate sacrifice needs to be remembered, lest they be forgotten. **Pam Makricosta**

An Eerie Tale of Brown's Island

THE UNNATURAL HISTORY OF BROWN'S ISLAND

Introduction to "The Unnatural History of Brown's Island"

Savannah Schroll Guz

The 1972 explosion at the Brown's Island coke plant affected my husband's family deeply. Among the many workers killed in the blast was my husband's uncle, Andrew Guz, who escaped the initial explosion but was killed upon going back in to render aid. Even though I never met Uncle Andy and my husband was still very young at the time of the tragedy, I still feel I know him. He maintains a presence in our home through photographs that hang in our kitchen and on the "ancestor walls" in our hallway. His kind eyes smile out in a bashful way from these black-and-white photos. It is his conspicuous absence from our later color pictures, the knowledge that he built the house that stands beside our own, and the stoic sorrow with which people refer to his passing that made me begin thinking about this island in the middle of the Ohio River. My husband told me about the island's lore, about the Native male figure people were said to have watched walk the metal bridge. I started to research and imagine, and the following story developed.

The title is a play on words. Some years before I came to Weirton, I worked in a building that housed a museum of natural history, and on my way to visit the staff photographers, I would regularly walk through hallways created by stacks of drawers in which the bones of early humans were organized. It was simultaneously fascinating and eerie, especially when the lights in those storage areas were turned off. As I was working on this story, I thought about the possibility that Brown's Island was a burial site for early Native peoples, that the island's soil held their bones, their artifacts, and perhaps even their lingering energy signatures. This history was not natural in any traditional sense, and so I titled it "The Unnatural History of Brown's Island."

The Unnatural History of Brown's Island

Savannah Schroll Guz

In the early autumn of 1803, Meriwether Lewis set foot on the muddy shore of an island between the rocky banks of western Virginia and the newly created state of Ohio. As soon as his feet caked with dense riverbed sludge, he felt, prickling across his consciousness, the peculiar sensation of being watched. Charged by President Jefferson with recording the national landscape's varied climate and extensive contours, Lewis felt he must now conform to the behavior of a scientist and employ more practical sensibilities. So he ignored his uncomfortable awareness and focused instead on setting up camp. He clipped botanical samples, pressing them between pages of his travelogue. And just before sunset, he caught a rabbit, built a fire, and set his damp boots to dry on the rocks around it.

The stars above the island's thick forest were at their greatest intensity when Lewis' fire finally lay in dying embers. He slept deeply for several hours and slowly woke to a sound he did not recognize. His logical mind, still submerged by exhaustion, thought that the men who were slated to join him on his trip south had unexpectedly arrived on the island. When his consciousness finally rose to the surface and his eyes opened, he thought: *I must get the fire going again.*

But what he saw as he still lay prone was neither William Clark nor any of the thirty enlisted men he would eventually meet in St. Louis. Around him on every side were Indians, but not in any conventional human form. They were like glass vessels filled with captive pipe smoke. Their substance circulated endlessly and looked a volatile blue-gray. These figures stood gazing at him, without speaking. He could see their distinctive features: their cheekbones, their crooked noses, their stoic eyes. They did not seem to indict him, but appeared to search the content of his fluttering insides. Lewis sat this way for several moments, stunned by fear, his heart pumping blood that went straight to his temples. When none of the Indians moved or appeared to threaten him, he rekindled the fire, alternately looking over his shoulder and bending to coax the flame into greater brightness.

The visions, but not the feeling, dissolved in the light. And despite heavy fog that settled on the island and continued several meters down the river in both directions, Lewis fled shortly before dawn, paddling forcefully upriver. He neither wrote about nor spoke of his experience to anyone.

It began to drizzle lightly as Ernest T. Weir, legs apart, umbrella poking the earth with grand decision, stood gazing over a precipice abutting the Ohio River. He was in a long woolen coat, fashionably cuffed trousers, and smart-looking high-waist silk vest. What he'd set his gaze on was the densely forested island that lay within the original acreage purchased for the steel company he brought up from Clarksburg.

"I'll tell you," he said to his assistant, who also looked out over the river, "we're going to start producing our own coke. If we want to compete with these giants, we've got to do it. Our cost overruns have just been too high." Weir pointed to the island with his long handled umbrella. "Now," he said, "that's the place right there. Let's get it cleared."

His assistant, an amateur historian, looked at Weir and said, "You know, that island has been marked by incidents of serious misadventure."

"What misadventure?" asked Weir, turning suddenly.

"About thirty years ago, three barges crashed into each other and dumped thousands of bushels of coal into the river."

"And what caused that?" asked Weir.

"They say it was the sandbar near the island, but I've read that the barge pilot only ran into the sandbar because he saw Indians standing along the island bank."

"Indians?"

"That's what I read."

"What other *misadventures*?" asked Weir, balancing his umbrella against his shoulder.

The man pursed his lips, thinking. "None other that I know of."

"One incident! One!" said Weir striking his umbrella against the ground. "Superstition is all, John. Pure superstition."

Nearly every tree on the island was felled within a week, and during that period, Weir had strange and unsettlingly palpable dreams, in which he was tied to trees by Indians wearing fringed leather breeches and deerskin mantles. Their faces bore fine red tattoos. Once the old man was firmly bound against the bark, the younger Indian males began swinging their axes at the tender, bloated abdomen beneath his nightshirt. Weir woke sweat-soaked and usually on the floor beside his bed, where he was often reaching out into darkness and pleading loudly for mercy. Once, while bathing, he even found what he thought were reddish bruises left by the ropes he dreamed had bound him.

This continued as the company began excavating for the foundation of the coke plant. Besides the tree roots, flinty anthracite, and viscous bitumen that darkened the island's soil, the workers began hitting pockets of bones. Femurs, splintered tibia, and finally a series of human skulls emerged from the soil. Five workers fled their posts as soon as word spread. One even dropped his shovel after it struck and broke a human mandible, scattering yellowish teeth over dirt crawling with earthworms.

"The men aren't happy," said Weir's assistant. "Several of them have seen an Indian Chief just a few feet from where they're digging. They're threatening to leave."

"Let them!" Weir replied, pounding his desk with a fist. "We'll find other men who want to feed their families." He was irritated by lack of sleep, which made him more impetuous than usual. Even his lip had taken to curling upward, to show the spaces between his ridged, ivory-colored incisors.

Most of the men engaged to work did stay, while others were brought in after fresh concrete covered whatever bones remained buried. The human remains initially uncovered during excavation were piled near a seam of cloudy quartz, which had ruptured the ground's surface about 300 meters west of the building site. The appearance of the quartz fascinated one or two of the workers, who reverently carried the bones to lay beside it. Eventually, however, the bones disappeared, and no one seemed to notice. Some were glad for their disappearance and asked no questions, assumed they were cleared away by other workers or carried away by animals. Others barely registered their existence in the first place and ignored the respect that some men—mostly immigrants—paid them. They were soon forgotten. The coke plant began cooking coal, and the bald, treeless island was alternately orange with oven fire or pallid grey from fly ash.

Weir again stood on the rocky precipice near the country club he'd begun constructing and looked at the pale red flame that shot eight feet into the overcast sky. Even at this distance, the acrid stench of burning coal was strong enough to choke a man.

"Smell that!" He inhaled deeply, smiled and stifled a cough. "Now that's progress! Progress without your misadventures, John. Eh?" Again he smiled at the man standing next to him, and in an uncharacteristic gesture of familiarity, nudged his assistant in the ribs.

Weir was no longer troubled by dreams of Indian braves. He slept soundly every night and made trips to Detroit and Washington and fought shop unionization for years. But the island remained a source of speculation. Indians were seen to walk across the wide, silo-shaped gas holders. Others lingered on the slick tin-roofs of the coal storage buildings. When workers saw them, the Indians threw what appeared to be spears, yet no spears were ever found on the ground.

Word spread about the island, and the more superstitious workers requested transfer back to the tin mill. Truckers refused to deliver loads there, having seen tanned men in fringed deerskin pants, feathered braids, and tattooed faces at the end of the service bridge connecting the island to the mill. Eventually, the plant and the surrounding area were overrun by rats, which crawled along duct work and pipes, cornered secretaries in the few plant offices, and got into workmen's lunch pails. They were bold and unafraid of the searing oven heat. And they were alleged to have issued directly from the moccasined feet of Indians sighted near the plant's permanent scaffoldings. When workers began setting jars of cornmeal and plaster of paris around each building's steel walls, the rat problem abated. But the Indians continued to appear at regular intervals for decades, particularly at night and in spite of the obliterating pink of the sodium vapor lights.

Two decades after Weir's death, the coke plant still plumed a foul-smelling odor that invaded buildings and reached even the metal desks of journalists at *The Weirton Daily Times*. But the odor was less pungent now, as a series of the coke ovens stood temporarily dormant.

—

The week before Christmas 1972, a feathery snow lay on Brown's Island. Cold froze the mud along the river bank and ice clotted its shallows. Five men from Koppers Construction stood in the plant's battery basement, inspecting the coke ovens for problems in anticipation of a January re-start.

A worker in dark canvas overalls and foam-lined rubber boots got on his knees to examine the flues that traveled across the oven floor. He smelled gas, but it was not stifling. More important to him was the conversation in the next chamber, where his co-workers were talking about going upstairs for coffee. He was about to declare his approval when he looked up and saw, gazing down at him, a dark-skinned male with braided hair, hollow cheeks and a hawkish nose. He was stripped to the waist, and around his neck was a pouch made of squirrel hide, the head and clawed feet still attached. It bounced gently against the arch of the man's rib cage.

The workman cried out and stumbled backward, trying to stand upright so he could run. But he fell against the bricks. The Shawnee Chief stepped closer. The men from the next oven came to the chamber doorway to see what Bowers was yelling about and also saw the chief, whose face carried red marks that looked like tattoos. The chief lifted his double-pronged eel spear, pointed accusingly at the men, and with a downward swing, scraped the flinty prongs against the oven bricks. Sparks flew.

At 9:44 a.m., the first explosion erupted from the battery basement, flinging bricks, steel girders, and slag fragments upward to levels above. Through the break room floor came charred fragments of five Koppers Construction oven inspectors, while the attendant heat caused the thin steel walls to begin folding. Men went back in with gas masks to rescue survivors, but found them burnt and missing limbs or under debris so heavy no human could move it alone.

While men searched for co-workers, two more explosions followed, killing everyone who went back to help. Fire raced through the debris, using every last bit of oxygen left and asphyxiating everyone still conscious. When a gas line broke, the island was sealed off, and rescue squads sat on the service bridge with their lights flashing.

In the decade that followed, fewer men would agree to work at the plant. It grew to have an ever more menacing aura. From 590 workers, only 275 returned after clean-up. The stories of Indians persisted and developed, with people claiming to see, at the end of the mill's long service bridge, a tanned figure bearing what looked like Poseidon's trident.

By 1982, the corporation closed the coke plant entirely, shutting down the 87 ovens and reassigning the remaining employees to mill jobs. The land was offered for sale, despite its heavily contaminated soil, but there were no takers. It now stands in the middle of the Ohio River emptied of trees, grey with pollution, marred by a rusting industrial fortress. Abandoned forklifts, mounds of coke, and oxidized outbuildings still litter the landscape. It is now a monument to the industrial pride that ignored human ritual and natural order. And as for the native spirits, no one disturbs them, so they do not appear.

Index

Symbols

Harris, Kenneth "Kenny" 52

A

Adovisio, Dr. James 122
Allen, Cyrus 188, 190
Andrew Guz 98
Andy Guz 88
Art Holsinger 7
Arthurs, Edward \ 89
Arthurs, Edward "Dick" 33
Asbestos Union #2 25, 37, 101

B

Badis, Eugene \ 72
Baker, Stanley 141
Barnell, Samuel 188
Bartgis, Rodney 122
Batts, Thomas 135
Beasley, David 162, 167
Belt, Rachel 170
Bensi, Charles 91
Bilderback, Margaret 174
Black, Clarence 11, 12
Black, Jim 11, 12, 71
Blanche 183
Booher, Bill, Dr. 96
Bordner, Wilson 91
Bowers, Charles 91
Bowers, John 60, 111
Bray, Howard 33, 89
Bray, Mercy 185
Bricklayers Union 24
Brown, Barry 91
Brown, George 159, 160, 168
Brown, Honor 158
Brown, Hugh 157, 158, 160
Brown, James \ 27
Brown, Margaret 159, 161
Brown, Rachel 159, 161
Brown, Richard 157, 159, 160, 161, 162, 163, 164, 172
Brown, Richard Jr. 159
Brown, Richard, Jr 161
Brown, Richard, Jr. 159
Byrne, Patrick 94
Byrne, Paul 40

C

Campbell, Duncan 165, 166
Campbell, James 162
Campble, James 164
Carpenters Union 25
Cashman, John, Dr. 111
Cayuga 133
Celeron (de Bienville, Bainville) 137
Celeron de Blainville (Bienville) 135
Clark, William 150, 154, 246
Clifford Lewis 123
Cline, Micki (Hervey) 66
Coking process 230
Coll, Fred 101
Cooper, James 175, 185
Cooper, Susan 185
Cooper, Wellington 175, 185, 186, 187
Cornstalk 143
Crawford, John 172
Cresap, Michael 141
Cronkite, Walter 108

Crowley 44, 90
Crowley, Michael \ 40

D

D'Annibale, Robert 59
David Javersak 203
Davis, Raymond 91
Decker, John 147
Delaware 134
Delf Nerona Museum 125, 128
Dorothy Holsinger 7
Doyle, Mary Jane 171
Dunmore, Lord 142
Duquesne, Marquis 138

E

Eafrati, Bernard 74, 77, 91, 110, 111, 114
Eafrati, Joseph 77
Edgington, George 144, 146
Edgington, George Jr 144
Edgington, Isaac 144
Edgington, Jesse 144
Edgington, John 144
Edgington, Joseph 144
Edgington, Thomas 144, 145
Ed Kliner 99
Ellicott, Andrew 149
Emily 182
Evening Review (East Liverpool) 107

F

Fach, Charles 55
Fallam, Robert 135
Ferguson, Cyrus 202, 204
Ferguson, Everett 7, 204, 205, 214
Ferguson, Mary Shakley 172
Ferguson, Richard 7, 30, 96
Fetzer, Elmer 126, 127
Flood of 1884 181

Flood of 1936 207
Flood of 1972 20
Fraser, Andrew 109
Frazier, Leo 91, 112

G

Gaines 95
Gaines, Robert \ 53, 89, 97
Gaines, Robert "Kenny" 32
Galanios, Deno 91
Garrison, Charlie 98
George Hamilton Company 90
George Rogers Clark 141, 150
Gerald Michael Pearson 52
Ghenne, James 91
Gibson, John 142
Girty, Simon 143
Glen Brady 26, 27
Grave Creek Archeological Complex 125
Greathouse, Daniel 142
Greathouse, Harmon 162
Greathouse, Jacob 141
Guz, Andy, Sr. 74

H

Harris, J.H. 110
Harris, Kenneth \ 50, 91
Higby, J. D. 107
Hinchcliffe, Basil 109
Hines, Steve 98
Historic Preservation Act 14
Historic Preservation Act of 1966 13
Holaday, Elizabeth 157
Holaday, Moses 157
Holliday, John 162
Holliday's Cove 144
Holliday's Cove 17, 145, 157, 158, 161, 162, 163, 164, 171, 189, 190, 203, 204, 209, 210, 235
Holsinger, Art 6

Index

Holsinger, Dorothy 241
Honor Brown 163
Hooker, Elizabeth 171
Hooker, Emanuel 171, 178
Hooker, Eurath 170
Hooker, George 171
Hooker, Iris 173
Hooker, John Randolph 171
Hooker, Levinia (Hindman) 173
Hooker, Margaret 174
Hooker, Margarett 188
Hooker, Mary Jane 171
Hooker, Minerva 171
Hooker, Richard, Jr. 170, 174
Hooker, Richard, Sr. 174
Hooker, Samantha 171
Hooker, Samuel 170
Hooker, Tallman 172
Hooker, Thomas 170

I

IBEW 246 26, 53, 89, 91, 102
Independent Steelworkers Union 114
Independent Steelworkers Union (ISU) 17
Iroquois 132, 133, 134

J

Jackson, Eliza 160
James Brown 33, 89
James Deganhart 111
James Tuttle 90
Javersak, David 158
Jefferson 150
Jefferson, Thomas 149, 245
Jemison, Mary 147
Jewett, Jeff 178
Jewett, Lewis 178
Jewett, Lorenzo 171, 178
Jewett, Mark 177
Jewett, Sumner 171, 177, 178
Jewett, Susan (Henry) 178

Jim Cunningham 28
John, Rodney 127
Johnston, Benjamin 157
Jones, Dennis 8, 15, 23, 76
Jones, Ronald T. 109

K

Keyes, Blanche (Stedman) 182
Kiefer, William 114
King, James 142
Kingsbury, Elezear 179
King's Creek 136, 225
Kinney, Molly 162
Kinney, Sarah 162, 163, 167
Kliner, Carole 99
Kliner, Ed 103
Kliner, James 99
Knapp, Patience (Jewett) 178
Knapp, William 178
Koppers 3, 3, 4, 20, 24, 25, 49, 51, 59, 61, 63, 66, 67, 70, 73, 74, 90, 93, 98, 99, 100, 107, 108, 109, 112, 113, 219, 250, 251
Kraina, Joseph \ 215
Kraina, Michael 7

L

Laborers Local 809 24, 51
La Salle, Robert 134
Lash, Raymond 28
Lenape 134
Lenape (d 134
Lenape (Delaware) 134
Levinia 173
Lewis, Andrew 143
Lewis, Clifford 123
Lewis, Henry 163
Lewis, John 165
Lewis, Meriwether 148, 149, 151, 152, 241, 245
Lewis, Sarah (Kinney) 162
Lewis, William 148

Logan 142
Logan (Talgayeeta) 133
Long, Charles 50
Long, Donald 50

M

Madden, Thomas 161
Makricosta, Pam 243
Martin, Lou 179
Maslowski, Bob 123
Mayer-Oakes, William 126, 140
Maze, Clyde 56
McCloy, Jack 35
McGinnis, Harry 187
McKenna, Ed 69
Meadowcroft Shelter 122
Meriwether, Lucy 148
Metz, Philip 109
Miami 133, 135
Michael Repko 44, 90
Micki Cline 68
Miller, Albert 122
Milsop, Thomas 12
Mingo 133, 135, 136, 142, 144, 147, 193, 213
Mingo Junction 134, 136
Miser, Art 187
Miser, Henry 185
Miser, Henry 186
Mitchell, Mary Lynn 7, 95
Mohawk 133
Molly Kinney 164
Moore, Arch 107
Moulton, Gary 152
Myers, Jacob \ 141

N

Native American Graves Protection and Repatriation Act 13
Nessley, Barbara 161
New York Times 73, 108, 193
Noe, Jeanne 58, 111

O

Ober, Fred 100
Ober, Russell \ 90, 100
Occupational Safety and Health Administration (OSHA) 110
Ogden, Gary 49
Ogden, Ross 50
Oneida 133
Onondaga 133

P

Palumbo, Francis 98
Panacci 231
Panacci, James \ 229
Paravano, Henry 54, 73, 109
Pat Byrne 93
Pawlock, Steven 64
Pearson, Christine 52
Pearson, Gerald \ 74
Peneschi, Joseph 112, 113
Petras, Bob 176
Phillips. J.A. 17
Pittsburgh Post Gazette 112
Pittsburgh Press 72, 219
Plumbers and Pipefitters 490 24
Pollard, Deborah (Hennis) 68
Poorman, Kenneth 91
Porter, Harry 22, 34, 36, 37, 38, 61, 104, 105, 106
Pratt, Ray 57
Press, Sanford 55

R

Redline, Jack 18
Reducah, Sandy 102
Richard Hooker 171
Richards, Dean 51
Riley family 146
Riley, James 146
Robbins, Chain 108
Robinson, Bill 8

256

Index

Runkel, Michael 7, 46

S

Stanley Anthony 71
Stedman, Emily (Jewett) 178

T

Tallman Hooker 174, 188
Tallman, Phoebe 171
Taylor, Samuel 185
Teasdale, Margaret 174
Templin, Harvey 60, 111
Thomas Jefferson 148
Thwaites, Reuben Gold 158
Toms, John 90
Tuttle Albert \ 44
Tuttle, Albert\"Al 90
Tuttle, James \ 44

U

U.S. Corps of Engineers 128

V

Van Sickle, David 25, 59, 67, 90
Van Swearingen, Andrew 144
Varney, Patience 177
Veraldi, Joseph 91

W

Washington, George 136, 139, 157, 241
Weimer, Dr. Bernal 123
Weir, E.T. 17
Weirton Daily Times 8, 25, 72, 109, 112, 143, 173, 199, 201, 208, 209, 214, 238, 250
Weirton Steel Bulletin 19, 21, 110
Welch, Jack 142, 161, 203, 221
Wellington, Mary 185
Wells, James 161

Weymouth, Thelma 59
William Penn 133
Wood, Thomas 135
Wyandot 145, 147

Y

Yenchochic, Marge 73, 74
Yobe Electric 30, 89, 95, 112, 113
Yund, Bill 42

Z

Zane, Ebenezer 141
Zielinsky, Tom 8, 225, 227
Zuros, Paul 155

Made in United States
Orlando, FL
02 March 2022